10 Days to Miracle Speech Power

Cathy Handley

Parker Publishing Company, Inc.

West Nyack, N.Y.

© 1978, *by*

PARKER PUBLISHING COMPANY, INC.

West Nyack, N.Y.

All rights reserved. No part of this book may be reproduced in any form or by any means, without permission in writing from the publisher.

Library of Congress Cataloging in Publication Data

Handley, Cathy
   10 days to miracle speech power.

   1. Public speaking. I. Title.
PN4121.H227   808.5'1   77-20685
ISBN 0-13-903260-6

Printed in the United States of America

*To That Fine Speaker
Elizabeth Doty*

WHAT THIS BOOK CAN DO FOR YOU

Create a business speech by recipe? Make a terrific talk not by luck but by a miracle 10-day plan?

That's exactly what *10 Days to Miracle Speech Power* gives you—a new and practical formula for planning and delivering a speech with big-league style . . . a blueprint for linking together a series of small miracle steps that mushroom into a smashing wonder talk!

This book embodies an innovative method to help business people in various fields become effective speakers.

An executive director's problem—dull delivery—was solved when he utilized this "miracle speech power" method of drafting and delivering a talk. What happened? He gave a talk that roused his audience from table-drumming to palm-pounding. And it resulted in his being elected president of a professional society, a long-time goal.

A 10-Day Speech Crash Course

Because of its step-by-step method, this is a talk cookbook that takes you from the moment you mark your calendar (after accepting a speech invitation) through a 10-day crash course of preparation and rehearsals to delivering a high-intensity talk.

Although the plan covers 10 days, you may wish to take more or less time. You can do so and still follow the flexible schedule.

What the Plan of the Book Is

Each chapter is one day of this 10-day plan for making a speech. During Days 1 through 6 you prepare your talk, using the latest tested methods, as well as effective short-cuts. For example, on Day 2 you make your listener hot sheet and check your subject for audience appeal.

On Day 4 you choose from five crash-course *patterns* to compellingly organize your talk. Then you quickly write it, using the race-car driver fun approach. *You don't do a lot of tiresome rewriting.*

On Day 6 you shape up your talk with "gut-feel" and anecdote-appraisal size-ups.

The Power-Planned Delivery

On Days 7 through 9, you shift from speech developer to performer with fascinating rehearsal workouts. These include utilizing Body English, plus home and business rehearsals that virtually success-proof your presentation.

Also, on Day 9 you gulp a four-ingredient gratitude cocktail that allows your natural speaking ability to surface.

On Day 10 you receive techniques for putting across your high-impact talk, including 12 "give-aways" and guides for conducting a Q&A.

Professional Pointers

Throughout the book you'll profit from 93 Pro Pointers that put the professional polish into your talk, for which a speechwriter or speaking coach might charge hundreds of dollars.

In-Control Tips

Especially valuable is the advice that enables you to master the mental obstacles such as work pressures and worry about your talk's reception.

At the end of each chapter are in-control tips to let you condition your mind before falling asleep so that "it works for you" to mould a winning speech.

Two Helpful Treasure Chests

The final chapters sparkle with two treasure chests of resource material—scores of *actual* openers and closers, subject ideas, as well as lively stories and wit which you can use to concoct a talk *without having to consult outside reference books.*

Preparing and delivering a speech that is high impact, highly professional and well-received is now as easy as counting from one to ten.

Cathy Handley

CONTENTS

What This Book Can Do for You 7

Day #1: **How to Go into 10-Day Training
for Miracle Speech Power** 17

Analyzing the Bottom-line Speaking Problem (17)
How This 10-Day Plan Works (18)
Must You Follow This 10-Day Plan Precisely? (19)
From Marking Your Calendar to Applause (19)
Fast-o-matic Breakfast/Subject Choice (20)
How Speech Ideas Surface (22)
This Book's Subject File: Idea Insurance (23)
Pushing the Hold Button (23)
Working Your Ranch of Information (24)
Jotting on Color-Coded Cards (24)
*Visuals? What Do You Already Have at Your
   Ranch? (25)*
The Miracle Bonus System (26)
In Control: Tips for Keeping Your Cool (27)

Flashback (27)

Day #2: **The Master Power Plan for Your Speech** 29

Two Planning Aids (30)
Time-Saver Audience Hot Sheet (31)
Testing Your Subject's Batteries (33)
*The No. 1 Decision: Is Your Speech Loaded with
   "You" Appeal? (34)*
The "Big Three" Speech Types (35)
How to Fascinatingly Inform (36)
Putting Real Fun into Entertaining (36)
The Blockbuster: Persuading Your Audience (36)

A Secret for Persuading Business Listeners (37)
Brushing in a Steering Sentence (38)
Drafting Three or Four Nutshell Points (38)
How to Track Your Visuals (39)
In Control: How to Forget so You'll Know More
   Tomorrow (40)

Flashback (41)

Day #3:   How to Use the Miracle Show-Biz Method   43

Daily Step-Takers (43)
Things You'll Need (43)
Clearing Your Desk and Laying Out Your Nutshell
   Points (44)
Adopting the Show-Biz System (44)
Shuffling Your Color-Coded Anecdotes (44)
Putting Down Your Quotes (45)
Slipping in Your Statistics Cards (46)
Analyzing the Fortune of Your Talk in the Cards (46)
Dealing a Note to Yourself on Things to Get (48)
If You Can't Find a Piece of Information—What
   the Pros Do! (49)
Three Tricks for Muscling Up Your Talk (49)
Odds-In-Your Favor Checking on Visuals (51)
How a Contractor Prepares a Background Sheet (51)
In Control: Putting Your Thought on "Humble" to
   Achieve Big Results (55)

Flashback (55)

Day #4:   How to Broad-Brush Your Speech
**   with Crash Helps 57**

Daily Step-Takers (57)
Things You'll Need (57)
Four Miracle Patterns (57)
   The Striking Story (58)
   Problem/Solution (58)
   The Big Gun (60)
   The Lasso (61)
Setting Your Thought Computer for a "Wow"
   Opener (63)
Reorganizing Your Cards (64)
10 Ways to Jump Your Talk Into Class A (64)
Steel-Trap Deciding on Your Opener and Closer (66)
Crash-Course Timing—Why Write Too Much? (67)
Writing Like a Race-Car Driver (68)
Keeping the Seven-Tenths Proportion (69)
Turning Off with a Mini-Reward (69)

In Control: Flagging Down Your Thought (69)

Flashback (70)

Day #5: How to Crash "Forget" Your High-Impact Talk— For Remarkable Results **71**

Daily Step-Takers (71)
Things You'll Need (71)
Forget Your Talk in Your Desk Drawer (72)
Forget Your Talk in Your Thinking (72)
Why You Need a Publicity Announcement (72)
How a Contractor Drafts a Publicity Announcement (74)
Look Over Your Background Sheet (77)
Shining It Up (77)
Nifty Nit-Picking (77)
The Power of a Picture (77)
Packaging Your Product (79)
In Control: How Your "I-Don't-Care" Attitude Can Strengthen Your Talk (81)

Flashback (81)

Day #6: How to Power Shape Your Entire Talk— From Zingy Opening to Punchy Closing **83**

Daily Step-Takers (83)
Things You'll Need (83)
Product Control (84)
Read Through with Your "Gut-Feeling" Glasses (84)
Make "I, S, F" Marginal Notes (85)
Zip Through with Your Anecdote-Appraisal Glasses (86)
Shift into Your Statistical Glasses for a Run-Through (87)
Slip on Your Quirky Glasses and Look at the Quotes (88)
Ten Guides for a Vital Talk (89)
Arranging for a Fast Tour (93)
Memorizing the Head and Feet (93)
Four Crash Checks on Your Speech Setting (94)
Relax, Relax, Relax (95)
In Control: Two "Pills" for a Strong Speech (95)

Flashback (95)

Day #7: How to Emerge Almost Miraculously As a Vital Performer **97**

Daily Step-Takers (97)

Things You'll Need (97)
Warm Up by Repeating the Memorized Head and Feet (98)
Work Out by Reading Your Speech Aloud (99)
How to Talk Off the Cuff (100)
Why You Must Follow the Crash Five-Minute Break (102)
Marking Your Talk Cards (102)
Five Aids to Eye-Power (104)
Weaving in Visual Aids (105)
Shadow-Boxing with Body English (106)
Work Out: Read Speech Through Once (106)
Be a Pumpkin-Changer (106)
Whipping Up Several Questions (108)
Delivering Your Introduction/Background Sheet/ Publicity Release (109)
Playing Before Your Home Audience (109)
In Control: Programming for Your Second Wind (109)

Flashback (110)

Day #8:   How to Fast-Play a Decisive Pre-Match 111

Daily Step-Takers (111)
Things You'll Need (111)
Three Concentrated Read-Throughs (112)
Tips for Using Visual Aids Smoothly (112)
Eight Guides for Using/Inventing Skilled Body Talk (113)
Inviting Business Friends to Play Audience (115)
Using a Critique Sheet (116)
Briefing Your Business Friends (116)
The Art of Turning On (118)
Your High-Intensity Pre-Match (118)
Fielding Q&A's (118)
Collecting Comments (118)
Assessing Your Strengths and Weaknesses (119)
Preparing a Q&A Notebook (119)
In Control: Score by Taking It Easy (120)

Flashback (120)

Day #9:   Little Miracle Workers Tighten Your Talk— And Your Inner Drive 121

Daily Step-Takers (121)
Things You'll Need (121)
Play Back Yesterday's Talk (122)
Make Any Necessary Changes (123)
Precision-Timing Your Talk (123)
Working Out with Miracle-Style Delivery (124)

Working Out with 80% Head-Up Delivery (125)
Clues for a Winning Q&A Session (125)
Buying Thinking Time (126)
Try Using the "How-Can-I-Help-You" Trick (126)
Follow These Stop-and-Go's (128)
Handling Hostile Questioners (128)
Foolproof Assembling of Your Visual Aids (130)
Like Your Inner Golf Game (130)
Allowed: A Four-Ingredient Gratitude Cocktail (131)
In Control: Setting Your Inner Thermostat
  for Success (132)

Flashback (132)

**Day #10: How to Employ Target-Hitter Tips
to Score a Winning Speech** **133**

Daily Step-Takers (133)
Things You'll Need (133)
Caution: Don't Rehearse More Than Three
  Times (134)
How to Shake "Ingratituditis" (134)
Three Guidelines to Turning Off at Work (134)
Two Aids for Inner Harmony (135)
Early Ducking-Out Advice (136)
Pro-Style Setting Up (136)
Being Well Organized Helps Your Credibility (136)
A Seminar Leader's Advice (137)
Mike Quickies (137)
Four Steps to Personal Warmth (138)
12 Give-Aways for Glow-Power (138)
Conducting a High-Impact Q&A (140)
Handing Out a Take-Away Kit (141)
Reaping Your Reward (141)
Should You Turn Pro? (141)

**Treasure Chest #1: Actual Titles, Ice-Breakers,
Bridges, Openers and Closers
for Miracle Speech Power** **143**

Titles That Spark Ideas (143)
Ice-Breakers (146)
Building Bridges (146)
Openers and Closers (150)

**Treasure Chest #2: Miracle Speaker's Reservoir
of Sparkling Stories
and Witty Words** **163**

Acknowledgments (212)

How to Go into 10-Day Training for Miracle Speech Power

The place: Los Angeles. The time: The start of the turbulent sixties. The late and great speaker Adlai Stevenson said: "When Cicero finished a speech, the people commented on how well he spoke. But when Demosthenes had spoken, the people cried out: 'When do we march?'"

This is a book for busy people who don't want to give empty speeches but who desire to do Demosthenes-style speaking *that gets results.*

Are you one of these busy people? Do you give talks oftener than just once every three years to your local Lions Club? And, if you speak from fairly often to frequently, do you yearn to do a top job? If you fit this description, good.

Pro Pointer #1: *10 Days to Miracle Speech Power* **can help you turn a speech that's weak into wonderful!**

Analyzing the Bottom-Line Speaking Problem

Today, when a person talks well, when he puts across his ideas persuasively, his career and his income move ahead.

However, the catch is: Many people give speeches but few give highly successful speeches. Why? Perhaps the answer lies in this little scenario:

> Place: Your office
> Time: 10 days before you give a speech
> Problem: How to pull together an outstanding talk in such a short time

> You feel nervous, palms sweaty, stomach muscles tightening. Your mind beep-beep-beeps: "Better get started—stop delaying—this is a pretty important talk—how do I put some topspin on it—what's the secret of adding special touches to make a standout talk—wish I had a speechwriter—maybe I'd better do research in the library—nope, no time!—I make talks that are okay, but how do I make a *super speech?*"

Your answer lies in the practical, step-by-step method in *10 Days to Miracle Speech Power.* It can help you turn out a blockbuster in as little as 10 days. What's more, this book is as simple to use as following a cookbook.

> Pro Pointer #2: This book will help you cut out many hours of wasted work, mistakes, amateurish results, and aid in bringing you significant career rewards.

How This 10-Day Plan Works

Recently I read an account of how Lyndon Johnson, 36th president of the United States, liked newspaper stories presented to him. He instructed an assistant to get as thick a red pencil as he could find. Whenever he discovered a story about Johnson, he told his assistant not to take time to read the story himself, but to circle each story in red, clip out the page, fold the story so it was on top, and have all the stories on Johnson's desk by six every day.

You'll note Johnson spelled out things in detail. As a busy person, I think you may wish similar specific shortcuts and details of preparing a talk. That's why *10 Days to Miracle Speech Power* spells out exactly *what, where,* and *when* you do various things in preparing and delivering a high-impact talk.

For example, on Day 1 in this exciting 10-day crash program you learn a little miracle worker: how to fast-choose an audience-gripper speech subject. On Day 2, you latch onto another miracle worker: how to crash draft your main points and craft a miracle steering sentence. On later days, you'll get blueprints for big-league polishing your talk. They are easy-to-follow instructions that today's "with-it" executives pay hundreds of dollars for in coaching sessions. And so you proceed in clear-cut steps through to Day 10, when you can deliver a speech to great applause and help put your business progress in high gear.

This 10-day plan will also detail when and where in the crash program you'll want to consult Treasure Chests 1 and 2 (the two final resource chapters) to obtain jokes, anecdotes, sparkling facts, even actual speech openings and closings you can insert into your own talk. To speed your progress, the crash plan gives you a brief list of Daily Step-Takers and Things You'll Need at the beginning of each chapter.

Must You Follow This 10-Day Plan Precisely?

No, your business situation is individual. While this book will give you a 10-day crash course in preparing and delivering a terrific talk, it's a flexible schedule. With *10 Days to Miracle Speech Power* you can take longer to put together a smashing speech. Or you can do it in less time. Merely make sure you cover the bases shown in the various chapters. But because this 10-day program is actually fun to follow, let's start out as if you must plan and give a terrific talk in 10 days. Who knows? One day you may wish to do so.

From Marking Your Calendar to Applause

1. Do you own a day-by-day desk calendar? Then, 10 days before your talk, with a red felt-tip marker *picture frame* each of these days with a heavy red line. These red-framed calendar pages will prod your memory every day to work on your talk.
2. To quickly remind yourself what you should do *each* day, mark each calendar page with an abbreviation of the

chapter heading from this book. For example, for Day 2, "The Master Power Plan for Your Speech," jot down "Master Plan."

3. Remember to follow the end-of-the-chapter tension-relieving in-control tips.

> **Pro Pointer #3:** The in-control tips are vital in helping you sparkle as a speaker.

Fast-o-matic Breakfast/Subject Choice

Since this plan uses the cookbook approach, we detail *everything*. So right now we're into Day 1 in whipping up your talk. And in our specific directives for Day 1, we advise you to stop at McDonald's, or your company cafeteria, pick up a Danish, coffee, juice and get in your office by 7:00 a.m. Why? To give birth to your speech idea early in the day.

Over a fast breakfast. "Over breakfast?" you yipe. Yes, for this reason. If you get your speech idea *early* in the 10-day program, you can then use the other days to flesh out your talk with zesty illustrations and rehearse and smooth it out.

> **Pro Pointer #4:** Taking too long to choose your subject is the biggest single sin in preparing your speech.

Just as you can't drag your feet in business, you can't drag them in any phase of putting together and giving a talk. Yet many people faced with 10 days to whip up a talk, waste eight or nine valuable days deciding on the subject, thus *insuring* they'll hatch not the speech "socko" but the speech "floppo."

> **Pro Pointer #5:** You can train yourself to decide on a fast speech idea almost automatically—and it'll be a fine one.

"Okay," you say, "but that word 'decide' bothers me. When it comes to a speech subject, it's not easy to make decisions."

Perhaps this story from the *Biblical Recorder* will show you how a bank president learned to make decisions. A young man interested in getting ahead went to talk to him and said:

"Tell me, sir, how did you become so successful?"

"Two words."

"And what are they, sir?"

"Right decisions."

"How do you make right decisions?"

"One word . . . experience."

"And how do you get experience?"

"Two words."

"And what are they?"

"Wrong decisions."

This story illustrates a point. Our business experience gives us something of tremendous value to impart to others. So, the first step in getting miracle speech results is to draw on speaking subjects right out of your own business experience or first-hand knowledge of a hobby.

But before you start searching your own background for a speech idea, take the lid off your coffee, take a bite of Danish, and *reflect.* Think hard about *who* your audience will be and *what* would interest them. Next, think about your own experience. What in your business experience will interest that audience?

As prompters, here are a few rough subject ideas which I find to be vastly appealing to business audiences:

- A new process
- A new procedure
- Improved methods
- Efficient procedures
- Time-saving tips
- Work-saving ideas
- Money-making advice
- Ways to attract customers
- Business-building aids

Audiences respond to talks about hobbies that describe:

- A new facet of the hobby

- How listeners can have more enjoyment (or better results) from the hobby
- How listeners can be healthier with the hobby
- How those in the audience can be wealthier with a spare-time hobby

Have some more coffee while you nail down those tentative ideas for your speech subject, *as they surface.*

How Speech Ideas Surface

Let's look at how two, not run-of-the-mill, but audience-enthralling speech ideas emerged. Here's how Jerry, a water well and pump contractor, comes up with an idea for a speech subject.

When Jerry receives an invitation to speak at a national convention of plumbing contractors, he runs through the above speech ideas.

Realizing his fellow contractors like tips for increasing business, it occurs to Jerry that his batting average for attracting new customers is high. He thinks, "Why not share tips on getting new customers?" And he notes this idea.

Observe how Jerry picks a tenative subject that will *snare* his listeners' interest. He avoids a low-interest subject like, "Plumbing Progress Through the Years."

Let's analyze another case history.

David, an architect, will speak to a women's club. They have asked him to talk on some aspect of his work. David knows he will speak to about 60 middle-income women from ages 25 through 60.

He has many things he could talk about, such as what makes good architecture—or how to work with an architect. But when he studies the preceding subject list, the word "new" jumps out.

He feels his newest venture, doing the design work for a restoration project of historical homes in the inner city, would be widely appealing. Especially so because the houses will sell to middle-income people (like his listeners) at reasonable cost, with unusually low mortgages available. He jots down the tentative idea: "Inexpensive historical homes."

Again, see the difference between major- and minor-league speech thinking. David resists going on an ego trip and talking about "My Most Exciting Designs." He targets his talk to grab his audience *right in their interest zone* by talking about what will fascinate not him—*but them!*

Like Jerry and David, you have many possible speech ideas out of your own experience. Put some of them down on paper.

This Book's Subject File: Idea Insurance

However, you may say, "I've got some inklings of ideas, but I'd like a little more idea stimulation." Then turn to page 144 which lists 27 titles of actual talks. If you read through these titles, you can often come up with a crash-course speech subject that's great.

For example, browsing through the list of titles of speeches, Jerry, the well and pump contractor, might see this speech title: "Selling Exotic Cars."

It might remind him that he sells a specialty, too—water pumps. His mental wheels spin and he pulls out a tentative speech subject which would have sizzle for his audience. The possible speech subject is "Selling Profitable Pumps."

Did you notice that Jerry and David did *not* finalize their speech subjects on Day 1? You don't need to either. But if you have put a possible subject on the back burner—fine! Your subconscious computer will take over. All day, while you cope with distribution, employee, and profit problems in your work, your "head computer" will be testing this subject, deciding whether it's okay to use it and sorting out ways (good stories, anecdotes, etc.) to make your talk come alive.

Pushing the Hold Button

By following the above steps on Day 1, you'll find it's only about 8:15 a.m. and you've decided on a subject. What do you do now? Tear into the day's work? No! Push down your mental "hold" button for the next 10 days. Mentally decide you'll hold off on initiating high-priority jobs, out-of-town trips, long lunches with friends, and family outings. In other words, don't entangle yourself in anything that takes extra thinking or physical effort. You want to give *everything* to preparing your talk.

Working Your Ranch of Information

Since it's still early and the rest of the office gang isn't around yet, let's round up a little material for your speech. We'll use this fun—but fabulously effective—method: working your ranch of information.

If you owned a real western cattle ranch, it might include cattle, riding horses, house, barn, and bunkhouse for your ranch hands. Your ample ranch might also include pastures, fences, machinery, roads, and cars.

Well, the miracle speech power method teaches that when giving a talk, you have an ample *ranch of information* about your business or hobby. You can use it to illustrate your talk.

If you owned a real western ranch, you'd ride around it, check on the fences, note the condition of your cattle, help solve a problem here or there with your ranch hands, perhaps pick up a tool you'd left someplace. You would find this very enjoyable.

You'll find it just as enjoyable to mentally ride your ranch of information—your business—with your rough speech subject in mind. Here's how to do it. As you mentally canter about

—you come to a file cabinet with a market survey which includes statistics you might corral;

—over there is another file cabinet with case histories stashed away;

—let your mental horse run a little and earmark a telling anecdote you read least week in a trade magazine;

—and mentally lasso a statement of authority in a newsletter.

By taking these mental trips, you save yourself time and energy; you find you have a surprising number of things to illustrate your talk; and you save yourself from going on a wild hunt to a library or panicked searching at random through your files or magazines for illustrative material. As you think of things that might illustrate your possible speech idea, make notes, but not on paper.

Jotting on Color-Coded Cards

Take 3 x 5 file cards in various colors (yellow, green, blue) and assign a color code. Perhaps:

Blue cards—anecdotes
Green cards—statistics
Yellow cards—jokes

Now, should you wish to follow the 10-day plan to miracle speech power in its pure form, break off and begin your regular work day. In the pure form of the 10-day plan, we *pace* ourselves. With proper pacing, you won't overwork on your talk on one day, then be too tired to work on it the next day.

> **Pro Pointer #6: In preparing your talk, do it in steps, rather than large time blocks for maximum "pow" results.**

And, of course, pacing can be done on your own timetable, too. If you wish to take longer than 10 days for putting together a talk, you may want to wait a day or two after getting your speech idea before you go into this next step.

Visuals? What Do You Already Have at Your Ranch?

Since we'll proceed by the 10-day plan in this book, take a few minutes after lunch. As you sit at your desk, again canter in thought around your ranch of information—your business premises or your home study—and think about visual aids to spice your talk.

You might mentally gallop over to your firm's engineering department—and spot professional charts you could borrow; then mentally canter over to the public relations department—perhaps you could uncover slides; a short ride to your own files might indicate you could rustle up absorbing give-aways—copies of articles your audience might relish. *Force* yourself to do this because the tendency is to say, "I'll think about visual material to illustrate my talk later."

> **Pro Pointer #7: An amateur keeps his amateur speaking status by not thinking on Day 1 about visual aids to illustrate his talk.**

So don't delay. On Day 1 write down ways you can illustrate your talk.

Jerry, the well and pump contractor, planning a speech before his industry associates, might note that he has

—good-quality color slides of jobs he's done which he shows prospective customers
—tear sheets of his newspaper ads.

Architect David, speaking to a women's club on good buys in historical homes, might indicate his possible visual aids as

—turn-of-the-century drawings of the houses
—architect's sketches of the renovated homes and revamped neighborhood.

> Pro Pointer #8: Often, you find you needn't go outside your ranch of information to get first-class visuals.

You're well along now in developing your talk with miracle speech power. So, again, if you follow the 10-day plan in pure form, pace yourself. Do the next step at home in the early evening.

The Miracle Bonus System

Suddenly you may say, "Hey, I've been working, riding around my ranch of information, collecting material for my speech. Will I be able to keep this up for 10 days?" Yes, if you start the 10-day bonus system. Decide on an overall bonus for yourself for making a good talk. Perhaps a new war history, sports book, or a boat accessory. Make it a definite incentive.

Letter this bonus across the bottom of each of the 10 days marked off on your calendar. If you have an ad with a picture of your bonus item, put it in your desk drawer or briefcase and look at it every day.

To keep your desire strong to make an outstanding presentation, figure out nine smaller rewards for the next nine days you'll be working on your speech. These mini-bonuses can be modest. If you like music, pick up a couple of records or cassettes. A gardening nut? Allow time to browse through a gardening catalog and select plants you'll order later. Like good eating? Snack on imported cheese and crackers one night, a choice fruit another.

A successful textbook writer I know sets up an amazingly simple bonus system—but it works! When he's read 50 pages of research, or has a rough draft of five pages written, he'll treat himself to a candy bar or a Coke. He sticks to his "production quota" until he's earned his treat. "It's surprising," he says, "how much *more* I get done with this reward system than without it " When he stops these small bonuses, his production drops off.

> **Pro Pointer #9: Don't allow yourself to enjoy your daily bonus till you do your day's stint in preparing your speech.**

In Control: Tips for Keeping Your Cool

While planning a talk and working out the mechanics of its delivery are important, *the most important single thing you can do in preparing a talk is to keep tension and anxiety under control.* So, beginning with Day 1 and through the next nine days, a special tip for keeping your cool is to refuse to think about your talk after 9:00 p.m. Absolutely turn off your speech in your mind. Late night quarterbacking of a talk is out.

How do you turn off your talk in your head? Think of a mental TV set. And picture yourself turning from a channel about your talk to another program. The trick is to replace the talk channel with engrossing but unstimulating thinking.

My friend Al, a public relations manager and ace speaker, says he turns to a thinking channel where he remembers hiking in a pasture as a teen-ager. He thinks about how the sun dappled a lake and how pleasantly the fish gleamed as they swished about. Thus, he unwinds and goes to sleep easily.

As you turn off your thoughts at night, remember to get to your office early the next day to painlessly plan your speech.

Flashback

1. To focus on a speech subject: (a) think about what interests your prospective audiences; and (b) what facts about your business or hobby will enthrall that audience.

2. "Crash" Idea Insurance: Read through the titles of talks in the back of the book. You'll *quickly* get lots of ideas for talks you can deliver.

3. Mentally ride about your ranch of information, spotting statistics, anecdotes, and case histories you may have in file cabinets, reports, magazine articles, or personal experiences which you can use to illustrate your talk.

4. Jot these ideas on 3 x 5 color-coded file cards—for example, use a yellow card for a joke, a green card for a statistic.

5. Mentally, keep cantering about your ranch of information and spot visual-aid possibilities—slides, graphs, drawings, etc.

6. Decide on a bonus for yourself—perhaps a new book or a golf club—for making a terrific talk. Then pick out some mini-bonuses (a delicious snack or a sports magazine) to give yourself every day. Make bonuses work for you so you'll deliver a superb speech!

DAY 2

The Master Power Plan for Your Speech

Famous trial lawyer F. Lee Bailey recounts that if he could do just what he wanted, he'd start his own school for trial lawyers. He goes on to say that in his projected live-in, one-year school he'd teach training in trial preparation, cross-examination, the use of polygraphs, and so forth. The point would be, says Bailey in his book *For the Defense* (Atheneum, 1975, with John Greenya), to make the school as *practical* as possible.

I have no doubt such a practical approach would pay great dividends in training trial lawyers. And, in fact, such a practical approach has been the way we've put together this 10-day miracle method for preparing a talk. This program leaves nothing to chance that can help you turn a talk from "sleepifying" to "electrifying."

Let's say you follow this 10-day regime in its pure form (though it'll work at your own pace, too). On Day 2, get into your office early, before the work-day begins. Put your portable breakfast on your desk. Take the cap off your coffee—and get ready to power plan your upcoming talk.

At this point, however, here's a little surprise for you. Get ready for a bit of pleasant operating help. From now on, through chapter 10, this book will give you two quick, handy planning aids.

Two Planning Aids

These planning aids are:

1. Daily Step-Takers—a list of *specific streamlined steps* you must take to produce a knockout talk.
2. Things You'll Need—recommended simple supplies that will help convert a speech from washout to "wow!"

In the following pages, these planning aids will be placed in boxes at the head of each chapter so you'll readily know what you'll do that day. You'll note, too, when you scan these aids how *easy* high-impact speech planning and preparation can be.

Let's look at Day 2's Step-Takers and Things You'll Need:

Daily Step-Takers
- Fill in the Audience Hot Sheet
- Craft a steering sentence
- Compose nutshell points
- Collect visual aids

Things You'll Need
- Ballpoint pens and paper
- Photocopy of the Audience Hot Sheet
- Various colored 3 x 5 file cards
- A briefcase, suitcase, or box for storing visual aids

Now, after you look at Day 2's Step-Takers and Things You'll Need, these steps and items for preparing your talk don't seem complex, do they?

Nor are they. Because the 10-day program is built on a principle a friend of mine, Frank, brought out to his ten-year-old son when he presented him with a fine pocket knife.

As soon as the thrilled lad received the knife, he began to whittle a piece of wood—producing the world's scruffiest bird. Then, Frank sat the youngster down for a few whittling hints. "Son," Frank said, "every piece of wood possesses a grain. If you go against the grain, you may mar the wood. But if you go *with* the grain, you'll find it much easier to whittle—and you can get handsome results."

The following miracle speech power Step-Takers will show you how to go *with* the grain in preparing your talk.

Time-Saver Audience Hot Sheet

One of the best ways to go with the grain, a *shortcut* way in planning your talk, is to use an audience hot sheet.

Audience Hot Sheet

1. Date of speech:
   Hour:
   Where:
   Length:
   Dress:

   Audience make-up
2. Name of group:
   Program director:
   Phone number:
3. Why is group meeting?
4. Age range of group:
   Sex:
   Education:
   Occupations:

   Audience attitude
5. Audience's recent knowledge of my subject (what have they heard in their own experience, meetings, read in trade journals, general publications, and seen on TV)?
6. Expected attitude toward my subject?
7. What will be the group's attitude toward me?
8. Should I avoid or be careful about any aspect(s) of my subject?

Basically, an audience hot sheet is an analysis sheet. It lets you *analyze* your future audience—their occupations, income, age, education, what they already know about your subject, and so forth.

About now you'll say, "Well, you mean my AHS is a marketing tool? It really pictures my future market for my talk?" Exactly. And it can be a powerful planning help.

Pro Pointer #10: Your AHS (Audience Hot Sheet) can help you prepare a talk in about 1/3 the normal time.

Here's how Marilyn, a speechwriter for a high-level Washington politician, used an audience analysis to produce a top speech for her client in only 10 days. Marilyn recalled:

"We had an ample budget, so I hired 12 people—young lawyers and homemakers with advanced degrees—to help me survey a cross section of people similar to those who would make up my client's audience.

"We found out their present opinion of my client, their reactions to several viewpoints he might express, and their own *wants*.

"We also noted what our future audience's income range, sex, education level, occupations, and so on would be like.

"It took us five days to make this audience survey, leaving me four days to write, polish, and have the talk typed, and one day for my client (an experienced speaker) to rehearse.

"The talk was cheered by the audience—and the press!"

Obviously, one of the reasons the talk rated cheers was that the speechwriter analyzed the future audience, prepared an audience hot sheet (analysis sheet), and worked from that.

You probably won't neet to make as deep a market analysis as Marilyn did to get a profile of your audience. In most cases, this crash program's AHS will work fine. So, on Day 2, quickly make a photocopy of this book's AHS, fill it in, and analyze what it reveals about your audience.

Testing Your Subject's Batteries

After you fill in your AHS and sit sipping coffee and thinking about whether your tentative subject will please that audience, you may decide your subject is A-Okay for them. However, remember what General Ulysses S. Grant said when asked to comment on success in war: "I do not believe in luck in war any more than I believe in luck in business." Therefore you can't rely merely on the findings of your AHS and *luck* to make sure your subject is absolutely on target for that audience. To make sure you've hit on an audience-gripper subject, test its batteries with these questions:

1. *If others speak on the same occasion, will anyone speak on the same subject or related subjects? If so, can I present an aspect that's new or different and worthy of my listeners' time?*
   Example: Jerry, the pump and well contractor, may find someone will also speak on wells and pumps. The other speaker's subject, "Equipping the Well and Pump Division," will differ from Jerry's angle—"How to Attract Profitable New Well and Pump Customers."
   Conclusion: Jerry's subject will test out as a strong one for a speech.

2. *Will I be able to handle any biases the audience may have about my subject?*
   Example: David, the architect previously mentioned who plans to speak about renovating historical homes, in considering audience biases, may discover a problem. Many audience members will feel that renovated homes in a ghetto district will not be *safe* to live in.
   Conclusion: David must make sure he can provide evidence—accounts of police patrols, special burglar systems in the homes—to answer this bias in the audience's mind, or his subject will test out weak.

So be sure to test whether your audience has a bias in regard to your subject, and either meet the bias, alter your subject, or choose another subject.

Let's say, however, your subject has tested out strong so far, and in fact, you think it may intrigue your audience. In that case, get ready to make the final, big decision.

The No. 1 Decision:
Is Your Speech Loaded with "You" Appeal?

Sex appeal plays an important role with the sexes, and *you* appeal plays a tremendous role in a speech subject. *You* appeal in a subject is somewhat like playwright James Barrie's comment on charm: "If you have charm, you don't need to have anything else; and if you don't have it, it doesn't matter what else you have." So, as you sit with your second cup of coffee judging your tentative subject, ask yourself: "Is my subject loaded with *you* appeal for this audience?"

Let's go back to our friend Jerry, the contractor who is going to speak to an industry group. After he chose his tentative subject, "How to Attract Profitable New Well and Pump Customers," Jerry might begin to have second thoughts.

His thinking might run: "I'll be addressing an industry group. Sometimes these fellows like subjects that concern the industry in general. Maybe I should speak on something like 'The Importance of Increasing the Supply of Plumbers for the U.S.' " The simple subject scoreboard I'll give you in the next paragraph can clear up Jerry's indecision and can help you as well.

Studies I have made of audience-appealing subjects show people are interested in, and in this order: (1) themselves, (2) their business, home, hobbies, (3) their industry, (4) their town, (5) their state, (6) their country, and (7) the world.

In ranking his "supply of plumbers" subject on this scoreboard, Jerry would observe his second-thought tentative subject would score in both the third and sixth places of interest for most people. Since he will speak to an industry group, he might even move these ratings up a notch. However, when Jerry checks his second-thought subject against his earlier proposed subject of "How to Attract Profitable New Well and Pump Customers," which would rate in No. 1 and 2 spots on the above chart, he probably would (and rightly) decide to go with a sure thing and choose the irresistible *you* appeal subject—"attracting profitable customers."

I can't emphasize enough to you the power of a *you* slant—hitting on a subject that helps your listeners function more effectively in their work, achieve more in a shorter time, make more sales, or increase profits. If it's an entertaining speech, then you must really entertain and amuse. If you speak on a hobby, you should tell your audience how it can make them healthier, more relaxed, happier, and so on.

So as you give your talk a final *you* test, think of a typical member of your prospective audience wearing eyeglasses. On the left lens is printed "help" and on the right lens is printed "me." *Help me!* That's what's hidden in the eyes of everybody you'll talk to.

> **Pro Pointer #11·** If your talk can answer the concealed "help me" in your audience's eyes, you can say, "Demosthenes, move over!"

If you follow this program in its 10-day crash form, you may wish to adjourn your planning and start the day's work. After lunch, you can spend a few minutes handling another step. But at any rate, whatever schedule you use, don't forget to p-a-c-e yourself for well-oiled results. Because the mind can't concentrate for too long at a time, three hard-nosed 30-minute periods a day can usually add up to better results than one several-hour planning session.

> **Pro Pointer #12:** A bonus factor in pacing yourself is when you take a break from planning your talk, your subconscious head machine continues to work, hammering out material. And, you find you get quality output with less effort.

The "Big Three" Speech Types

Once you decide you've hit on a real audience-arouser subject, this crash-course program advises you to determine what *type* of talk you'll give. So, while you have a sandwich lunch at your desk or take a few minutes afterward with your speech folder, decide whether you'll want to deliver a talk to:

- Inform

- Entertain
- Persuade

Sometimes it's a combination of two of these points. You may wish to inform and persuade your audience at the same time. Example: A company's general manager informs his staff about new procedures but he also wants to gain their support for them.

How to Fascinatingly Inform

A magic trick in putting over an informative talk—where you tell someone about a new process, method, hobby, and so on—is not to cover too large a scope.

Think of your subject as a sun, with rays of light radiating out from it, something like this:

Important: Don't plan to tell everything about your subject. Tell just one *ray* or aspect.

Putting Real Fun into Entertaining

Sometimes, as you contemplate planning a talk, you realize you want to *entertain* your audience. For example, if you make an after-dinner talk, its main purpose is often to entertain. If you plan to entertain your audience, *stay alert* from now on to collect entertaining material (jokes, anecdotes, humorous case histories, and so forth) and ways to present this material in a fresh and diverting manner.

The Blockbuster: Persuading Your Audience

However, today, the talk that often seems most in demand is the *persuasive* speech. Consider carefully and decide whether or not you'll make a persuasive speech. For example: Your speech might persuade employees to adopt a new policy . . . or convince an audience that your business has credibility . . . or lead local voters to elect you to the school board.

> Pro Pointer #13: The ability to deliver a persuasive speech accounts for many people sprinting, instead of poking, up the ladder.

If you decide your subject will make a good persuasive speech, begin now to think about a vital secret of persuasion.

A Secret for Persuading Business Listeners

In planning a persuasive speech, you must plan now to:

Establish a common bond. In other words, you must start thinking about what points you have in common with your audience. You'll want to mention these in your talk.

Example: Some years ago, a man born with a silver spoon in his mouth, who'd graduated from law school but had little business experience, was running for a high elective office.

Out on the campaign trail, he found it difficult to establish a common bond with his hard-working audiences, suspicious of him because of his short work experience.

One day, though, the young politico hit on a great gambit. He kicked off his talk to hard hats by recalling one time when he stood at a factory gate, shaking hands with workers streaming out at quitting time.

Talking to a wizened little man who said he'd worked on one machine for the last 30 years, the politician said, "Well, I'm afraid I don't have your work experience . . ."

The worker interrupted him, "You haven't missed a damn thing!"

When the society scion told this story to his blue-collar audiences, they exploded with laughter and from then on accepted him as an all-right fellow.

So begin now to ponder a common bond or two that you can bring up in your persuasive speech. Often, it can be as simple as: (a) You attended the high school in whose auditorium you're talking, (b) As a teenager you hunted near the factory where you're speaking, and (c) You're happy to talk in this fine city where your sister makes her home.

Brushing in a Steering Sentence

At this stage in the 10-day crash program, now that you know whether your talk will be informative, entertaining, persuasive—or a combination of these, let's build a steering statement for your speech. This compass statement is merely a complete sentence about what you'll cover, or where you'll go, in your talk.

For example, Jerry, the previously mentioned contractor, talking on how to attract profitable well and pump customers might put together this steering sentence: "You can attract profitable new well and pump customers three ways—knocking on doors, pleasing present customers, and advertising."

Architect David, talking about the historical home renovation project, might compose this steering statement: "Today I'll describe three reasons why one of these renovated homes can offer you a remarkable and money-saving opportunity."

After you note your steering sentence, you may want to break for work. Then at the end of the day take a few minutes for . . .

Drafting Three or Four Nutshell Points

You'll want to determine three or four main points you'll make in your talk.

To facilitate this, and to prevent getting lost in a sea of scribbled words, use the bottom of a coffee mug or drinking glass to trace four circles about 3″ in diameter on a sheet of paper. Now think of these circles as "nutshells." Write one main point you'll bring out in your talk on each paper nutshell.

> Pro Pointer #14: For a successful talk,
> confine yourself to making three or
> four main points—not half a dozen.

In the earlier analogy of the well and pump contractor, Jerry, in planning his talk, might decide to focus on three main points. He might write:

- "I get many new customers by contacting the owners of new homes under construction."
- "I've found *satisfying* my customers brings me many profitable referrals."
- "Properly handled advertising has proved another good business-getter for my firm."

Jerry would then look critically at his nutshell points. Because he wants his talk loaded with *you* (listener) appeal, he'll refine these nutshell points and make them listener-slanted. For example:

- "*You* can get many new customers by contacting the owners of new homes under construction."
- "*You'll* find satisfying your customers can bring you many profitable referrals."
- "Properly handled advertising will prove another good business-getter for *your* firm."

Here's how one of Jerry's nutshell points would look:

The architect will use similar *you*-slanted nutshells. And you can, too. So craft *your* nutshell points.

How to Track Your Visuals

Yesterday, on Day 1, as you mentally rode your ranch of information, you jotted down a few ideas for visual aids that popped into your head. By now, more ideas for visual aids have probably surfaced. So today, and if need be the next couple of days, force yourself to *button up* arrangements for your visual aids.

Here are some tips on how to do so:

- *As soon as* you decide to use a visual aid, put it into a briefcase, suitcase, or box. If you don't tangibly round up your visuals till the day before your talk, you often fail to

get them all together. And as one experienced speaker said, "You then *insure* the failure of your talk."
- *Right now,* collect any visual aids that are ready to use.
- *Make arrangements* for slides to be made or charts drawn. Remember, it takes several days to secure a photographer and get slides processed or to give an artist a chart assignment. So make arrangements in the next day or two.

On your visual aids, remember to:

- Make them *big* enough so everyone in the audience can see them.
- Use *good-quality* visual aids—no blurry slides, no faint, over-crowded or complex charts.
- Employ a *variety* of visual aids—for example, you may use charts, but don't make *all* your visuals charts. In your mix of aids, you might wish to include slides, blackboard drawings, and hand-out notebook material.

> Pro Pointer #15: Visual aid *variety* zips up a speech and helps make it major-league quality.

Now, let's stop speech-planning. Instead, go home. Relax with your family. But beware of a mid-evening danger. Around 9:00 p.m. don't give in to speech-planning panic. Don't let your mental wheels spin about points to make in your talk. Remember, in this crash program for miracle speech power one rule is that *you don't think about your speech after nine at night.*

In Control: How to Forget so You'll Know More Tomorrow

At the end of Day 2, resisting the urge to think about your talk calls for a stronger turn-off-your-thought prescription than yesterday. So here's Day 2's thought-control method.

Think about a successful accomplishment of yours in the past—a fishing tournament you won, a job you did that the company applauded, a community project you managed well. Dwell on this accomplishment. Go over every detail—how you did it, the great cooperation you got from others, how well everything worked out, the praise you received. Later in the evening drop off quietly to sleep.

However, if you still feel stimulated and tempted to think about your talk, try this mind slow-downer. Read a few poems or biblical psalms. This will help you wake surprisingly fresh. Your subconscious head machine will have had an opportunity to come up with ideas. And you'll be ready to rip into Day 3 when you learn to add a little miracle-power show biz to your talk.

Flashback

1. Fill out the Audience Hot Sheet and note if your subject will seem attractive to that audience.
2. To further test your subject, ask yourself if your talk will be interesting, helpful and/or profitable to your listeners—in short, will it have *you* appeal?
3. Decide whether you'll make a talk to inform, entertain, persuade—or a combination.
4. Compose a steering sentence that tells what you'll talk about.
5. Cut out three or four "nutshells"—paper circles about 3" wide. Write a main point of your speech on each nutshell.
6. Collect any visual aids that are ready to be used in your talk in a briefcase, suitcase, or box. Plan to complete other visuals you'll need.

How to Use the
Miracle Show-Biz Method

Daily Step-Takers
- Lay out your nutshell points
- Deal your anecdotes, quotes, statistics
- Check your visuals
- Prepare a background sheet

Things You'll Need
- Cleared desk
- Yellow legal pad and ballpoint pen
- A recent resume
- Any biographical notes about yourself from a company or external publication

---

On Day 3, when you get to your office early with your Danish, juice, and coffee, you may suddenly not feel like going ahead with planning your talk. You may feel a strange sensation—not hunger, your portable breakfast takes care of that. It's a sensation the following scenario points up:

First man: Say, pal, there's only one thing that keeps me from belting you.

Second man: What's that?

First man: Fear.

On Day 3, the only thing that keeps you from plunging into preparing a top-drawer talk is *fear*. Even if you're an experienced speaker, fear washes over you. Just as you begin the actual steps of planning your talk, fear whispers: "Maybe I shouldn't work on my talk right now. Possibly I should take some more time to think about my subject. Though I'm down at the office early, perhaps I should review the list of customers I'll call on later in the day." To lick this negative thinking, *10 Days to Miracle Speech Power* uses the following great way to plan your talk.

Clearing Your Desk and Laying Out Your Nutshell Points

Get everything off your desk. Swing your chair around till you face a short desk end. Now take out the nutshell points you prepared on Day 2 and lay them in a row along the desk end nearest you.

Adopting the Show-Biz System

A well-known fiction writer maintains, "I don't think of myself as writing novels. I think of myself as preparing *entertainment*." You, too, are preparing entertainment—you're in *show biz*—when you give a talk.

You'll recall that on Day 2 you jotted illustrative material on 3 x 5 file cards—anecdotes on blue, statistics on green, jokes on yellow and quotes from authorities on pink cards. Take out these color-coded cards. Since yesterday, you may have made notes about other things that occurred to you. Transfer this material to the appropriate colored cards.

Shuffling Your Color-Coded Anecdotes

Read through your blue cards and see which anecdote fits which nutshell point.

For example, Jerry, the contractor mentioned earlier whose

talk is tentatively titled "How to Attract Profitable New Well and Pump Customers," might find this blue card:

> Customer I serviced showed me my installation was faulty. I dug a new 450′ well with no charge to customer. Pleased, he recommended me to six friends. Result: Six juicy contracts.

Jerry puts this blue card behind his nutshell point: "You'll find satisfying your customers can bring you many profitable referrals." Then Jerry puts his other blue cards behind the appropriate nutshell points.

His desk top looks like this:

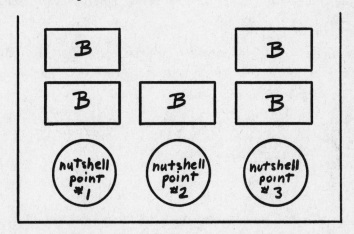

Note: In this and future diagrams, B stands for a blue card (anecdote), Y for a yellow card (joke), G for a green card (statistic), and P for a pink card (quote).

Putting Down Your Quotes

With all your anecdotes distributed behind your points, take your pink quote cards and place them behind the appropriate nutshell points.

For example, Jerry takes a file card with the following quote from Calvin Coolidge:

Press On
Nothing in the World Can Take the Place of Persistence. Talent Will Not; Nothing Is More Common Than Unsuccessful Men with Talent. Genius Will Not; Unrewarded Genius Is Almost a Proverb. Education Alone Will Not; The World Is Full of Educated Derelicts. Persistence and Determination Alone Are Omnipotent.

He places it behind his nutshell point, "You can get many new customers by contacting owners of new homes under construction." If other quotes from authorities have occurred to you, transfer them from your pocket notebook or your files to the pink cards. Then deal them onto the desk behind the right point.

Slipping in Your Statistic Cards

Now take your green (statistic) file cards. Also transfer any new statistics you've run across onto green cards. Slip them in behind the right nutshell points.

Analyzing the Fortune of Your Talk in the Cards

At this point, don't nitpick in judging your illustrative material. First, simply cast your eyes over the colored cards.

Pro Pointer #16: Do you see a *mix* of blue, green, yellow, and pink cards?

If you do, good! If you don't see a mix of four colors, but see only one yellow (joke) card and all the rest green (statistic) cards, you'll need to stop right now and get more yellow cards, as well as blue (anecdote) and pink (quote) cards. And, you'll probably want to weed out your green cards. You want a *salting* of statistics in a talk. Too many statistics come off as bad as too much salt on your roast beef—bitter.

Next, take a second reading of your color-coded cards. Does one nutshell point have only one color card behind it? To illustrate: Do you see four yellow file cards and no other color behind one nutshell point? Usually, it's best to see at least two colors behind each point.

Now, look again at your color-coded mixture. Are you especially *strong* on blue (anecdote) and yellow (joke) cards? That is highly desirable.

Pro Pointer #17: Anecdotes and jokes are box-office hits with listeners.

Here's how your cards might look on your desk top.

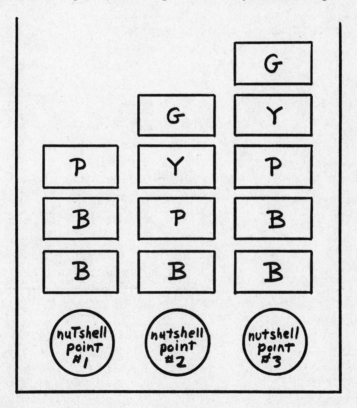

> Pro Pointer #18: Note that as you lay
> out your cards you'll pull out *more*
> material than needed. Later you can pick
> and choose the strongest material.

But you may wonder, "Is it worth the extra effort of collecting
more illustrative material in order to keep the most appealing and
discard the less appealing?" I've found it pays, pays, pays. In fact,
when I'm rounding up *plenty* of color-coded cards, I often think of
the fashion buyer anxious to move ahead.

One day she said to the powerful merchant prince of the
department store chain she worked for: "Would you tell me what
is the greatest secret of your success?"

"I don't have one simple secret," said the merchant. "All I
can advise is if you want success, you must *jump* at your opportunity."

"But how can I tell when my opportunity comes?" persisted
the buyer.

"You can't," barked the owner. "You have to keep jumping."

> Pro Pointer #19: This generous gathering
> (and later editing) of your
> color-coded material will help you to
> keep jumping at your speaking
> opportunity. It will aid you in delivering
> talks that don't rate as ordinary but
> outstanding—the kind that lead to
> prestige, promotions, power.

Dealing a Note to Yourself on Things to Get

As you look at your color mixture on your desk, you may see
you need more statistics or anecdotes to round out your
illustrative material. Make a note of these needs. Next, put away
your nutshell points and file cards in your desk.

> **Pro Pointer #20:** Don't try to decide now in what *order* you'll organize your file cards behind your points.

If You Can't Find a Piece of Information—Do What the Pros Do!

After lunch, consider your yellow legal pad notes. What information do you still need? If you can get it easily in your office, do so. If you can't easily lay your hands on it, do what the pros do: *Get something else.*

> **Pro Pointer #21:** Often, you save hours of time by switching to another anecdote, quote, or statistic instead of hunting for a special one. And the replacement may even be better!

Three Tricks for Muscling Up Your Talk

The fifth century B.C. philosopher Lao-tzu said, "The wise man does not lay up treasure. The more he gives to others . . . the more he has for his own."

Following are some ways to get more illustrative material to add to your talk's usefulness for others—as well as to help increase your reputation as a speaker.

Muscle Tip #1.   Check Treasure Chest 2 in the back of the book. You'll see an array of numbered sparkling stories and witty words.

Example: Contractor Jerry might discover #15 which says:

15   William Wrigley, the chewing gum tycoon, placed great
      faith in advertising. He expressed his advertising
      philosophy as: "Tell 'em quick—tell 'em often."

Jerry decides to paraphrase this. So he jots down the number of the anecdote on a pink card and the way he'll use it:

> 15   I agree with chewing gum tycoon William Wrigley
> who placed great faith in advertising. His rule of
> advertising was, "Tell 'em quick and tell 'em often."
> That's why I run a five-line ad once a week in four
> newspapers and . . .

As you browse through Treasure Chest 2, you'll find numerous items you can use.

Muscle Tip #2. Get hold of audience-related material that you can work into your talk. *Example:* Jerry, the contractor, phones the program director of the meeting where he'll speak and learns that about 10 of his prospective listeners already offer a well and pump service. He gets their names and also finds that about 30 more members have indicated on their questionnaires they'd like to go into water programs.

Therefore, Jerry plans to say: "I understand Clark Angler, Harrison Franklin, Bill Butz, Marge Miller (he names the others) already offer pump and well digging services, and that 30 or more of you would like to offer this service. So, I believe my experience can help you."

This recognition of the desires of the audience members—this speaking directly to the "help me" that's in the audience's eyes which I mentioned on Day 2—will make your talk much more effective.

> **Pro Pointer #22: Dig out material related directly to your listeners to *zoom* your talk's audience appeal.**

Muscle Tip #3. Plan to distribute hand-out material, such as photo-copied information sheets, surveys, magazine articles, company brochures, samples of your company's products, etc.

> **Pro Pointer #23: I find that listeners remember about eight times more vividly, and approvingly, the speaker who gives them hand-out material.**

While you need not decide firmly today (Day 3) what audience-related or hand-out material you'll work into your talk, decide *now* to use some. Then your mental computer will start working on its own, sorting out ideas. Later when you need specific ideas for hand-out material, it won't be hard to come up with them.

Odds-in-Your-Favor Checking on Visuals

Also after lunch, look into the progress of your visuals. Sometimes, an inquiring phone call prompts a supplier who forgot to look at his "rush" sheet to get going and get a visual aid to you. Keep checking and asking for your visual material every day after lunch, till you have it all.

> Pro Pointer #24: Failure in obtaining good visual aids lies in taking the line of least persistence.

How a Contractor Prepares a Background Sheet

At the end of your day, before you leave for home, grab a Coke from the office machine and enjoy a fun break by preparing two things to give to the program chairman:

1. A background sheet about yourself.
2. An actual introduction to your talk. If he so desires (and many do!), the program chairman can use it to introduce you to the audience.

To make the background sheet, run off a photocopy of the form shown at the top of page 52 and fill in your answers as Jerry Bascomb has done in his background sheet, shown on page 53.

Background Sheet

1. Name:

2. Present position:

3. Type of business:

4. Past position:

5. Title of talk:

6. Educational background:

7. Extra-curricular activities:

8. Publications:

9. Honors/achievements:

10. Significant audiences I've spoken to:

Background Sheet

1. Name: Jerry Bascomb

2. Present position: President, Jerry Bascomb, Inc., Pacetown, N.C.

3. Type of business: Contractor for water wells and pumps.

4. Past position: Independent digger, associated with Carlson Contractors, Pacetown, N.C.

5. Title of talk: "How to Attract Profitable New Well and Pump Customers."

6. Educational background: B.S. (date), Fawson University, Main Town, N.C.

7. Extra-curricular activities: President of the Pacetown Jaycees (date).

8. Publications: Co-authored "How to Dig a Water Well," 32-page manual, Bullfrog Press (date published).

9. Honors/achievements: "Chesty" award for top fund-raiser, Pacetown.

10. Significant audiences I've spoken to: Participated in several of this group's seminars.

You'll note Jerry decided to keep his tentative title. He feels it will *lure* his prospective listeners. However, a speaker will often shorten and snap up his tentative title to give it more appeal.

Here's how Jerry utilizes his background sheet to prepare his introduction to the audience which will be read by the program chairman.

Introduction

Today, I'm happy to present our next speaker who holds a B.S. degree from Fawson University in North Carolina and has conducted this association's well and pump seminars . . . real sizzlers!

Three years ago . . . coming down with a bad case of avarice and greed . . . he started his own highly profitable company, Jerry Bascomb, Inc.

Now Jerry's going to tell us a few of his money-making tactics with "How to Attract Profitable New Well and Pump Customers." Our own avarice-and-greed expert . . . Jerry Bascomb.

Note the manner in which Jerry introduces humor.

> **Pro Pointer #25: Poking fun at your most significant accomplishment is often a deft way to add humor in your introduction.**

It's also professional to give the program chairman your background sheet or resume. He may wish to pick out certain facts he can build witty remarks around.

Usually, you find writing your background sheet and introduction goes fast. So, now, with these completed, head for home and plug in to another part of the Miracle Speech Power method . . . turning off your thinking about your talk.

In Control: Putting Your Thought on "Humble" to Achieve Big Results.

A famous tennis coach once said he achieved better results when he taught his students to become more *humble,* and *not* to feel they must go out and play like demons *to win.* "Stop trying to win," he said. "Just go out and play as well as you can and really have fun!" The result of this new humility was they (1) had more fun and (2) won far more often, too.

Business people tend to feel they *must* make a blockbuster talk. And with this "must" in mind, they *destroy* themselves as speakers. How? They tighten up, work too hard (with wasteful, uncoached efforts) preparing their talk, don't relax enough, sleep too little, and end up *striking out* on the podium.

So now in this Miracle Speech Power crash course, listen to your coach. Think of yourself as *humbly* trying to express your native ability. Recall the reasons for giving your talk: (a) to help others, (b) to pass along useful or entertaining information, and (c) to be humbly willing to express your own talents.

This humble motivation will relax you. Think also about how *grateful* you are that you were able to take the necessary steps today in readying your talk. And think briefly about this: That tomorrow, Day 4, will be an exciting one because you'll find the *pattern* of your talk unfolding—the pattern that will make your talk different and *fascinating* for your listeners. But, remember, after 9:00 p.m. don't think about tomorrow. The rest of the evening do something relaxing, such as reading a sports magazine or playing a game or two with your family.

Flashback

1. To quickly deal your talk ingredients, clear your desk, sit at a small end and lay down your nutshell points—the main points of your talk written on small circles of paper.
2. Behind these nutshell points lay out your color-coded file cards—anecdotes, statistics, quotes, jokes, each category on a different colored file card.
3. Do you see a good *mix* of colors in the cards? Note if you need any further illustrative material and get it.

4. A handy place to find such material is Treasure Chest 2 in the back of this book. Consult it for witty words and sparkling stories.
5. Visuals? Keep riding herd on yours.
6. Fill out a photocopy of the Background Sheet in this chapter.
7. Using this background sheet, quickly write an introduction of less than 100 words to your talk. (This will be used by the program chairman to introduce you to the audience.)

DAY 4

How to Broad-Brush Your Speech with Crash Helps

Daily Step-Takers
- Choose a pattern
- Make a firm decision on your opener and closer
- Crash-course drafting
- Savor a mini-reward

Things You'll Need
- Lined yellow legal pad
- Ballpoint pen
- Red felt-tip pen

On Day 4, when you get into your office with your Danish-coffee-juice combo, how do you plan a speech so it'll sound unique? Fascinating?

One way: Use a compelling pattern.

Four Miracle Patterns

Here are four miracle patterns. You can utilize one of them in your upcoming talk.

The Striking Story

A winning pattern for a talk is to kick off with a striking story, joke, or brief case history. I think of the striking-story pattern as similar to the teaser at the opening of a TV program. Often, the more fascinating or pertinently humorous the opener, the better.

Here's how Jerry, the contractor, might start a striking-story pattern:

> The other day I was making a house call, seeking new business, and I overhead two youngsters talking. One said, "You've got a real nice kitty. I've asked my Dad and Mom over and over for a kitty and they always said no."
>
> The owner of the kitty spoke up with great authority and said, "Tommy, you don't know how to ask. I started asking for a baby brother, so when I finally asked 'em for a kitty they said yes right away."
>
> Believe me, friends, in getting new customers there's nothing like *asking* for business, from the right people, in the right way.

Here's how this striking-story pattern looks in picture language:

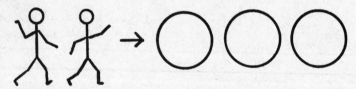

The figures indicate the opener. Note in this and the following patterns: (1) The arrow stands for the steering sentence, (2) the circles represent nutshell points, and (3) remember that each nutshell point is followed by illustrative material from your color-coded file cards. Later, I'll show you how to add a zingy closer.

Another winning pattern is the . . .

Problem/Solution

What a dynamic pattern this is for business people!

All of us face problems with our business, hobbies, civic and church work. When a speaker describes a problem that nags his listeners, and indicates he has a solution, this hits his audience as if learning one of their stocks rose 20 points that day. *The audience comes alive!*

The problem/solution pattern kicks off with a dramatic opener (statement, anecdote, example, case history, joke or statistic) about the problem. Notice, I said *dramatic* not drab.

For example, our pal Jerry, the contractor, does not drone:

> Today I want to tell you how I solved the problem of maximizing the market potential for expanded activity in North Carolina, and the consequent increase in renumeration from the patronage of various individuals that I contacted in a business way.

Obviously, this foggy statement *hides* the problem so the audience does not come alive. However, our friend Jerry isn't up there to slip his audience a verbal Miltown. Instead, he reaches for a *dramatic* presentation of the problem he'll talk about: attracting profitable new customers.

For example, Jerry might say:

> Three years ago, when I started my company, did I need business? I'll tell you how much I needed business. See these pants? (Holds up a pair of jeans with patches on the patches.) My wife kept patching these for me. I was putting every cent I could borrow from the bank into new equipment and to meet the payroll till the business started rolling in.
>
> And it did roll in because . . .

He then continues the problem/solution pattern.

In picture talk, I think of this problem/solution pattern as looking like this:

The "P" stands for posing the problem in the opener. The nutshell points (and their illustrations) represent the solution.

However, remember what we said about the problem opener being dramatic? In *my* mind's eye, I always see the problem/solution pattern as:

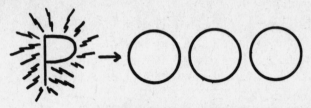

> Pro Pointer #26: The problem/solution pattern helps to put a few calluses on applauding listeners' hands.

The Big Gun

Often, a great way to start your talk is the big gun—making your strongest point first. In fact, because people frequently leave meetings early, more and more speakers use this pattern of placing *first* the most important thing they want to say.

For example, Jerry, the contractor, may plan three nutshell points—three methods of gaining new business. But because he feels that about 90% of his new business comes from knocking on doors of new-home builders, he'll stress that and give it first position and lion's share emphasis in his point line-up. In a 15-minute speech, he might spend nine minutes on his big-gun opener/first nutshell point and six minutes on the other two points and the closer.

The powerhouse big-gun pattern looks like this:

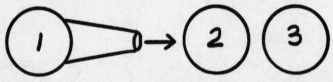

Note: The first main point is merged with the big-gun opener. This means, in Jerry's case, the steering sentence (arrow) will point to *two,* instead of three, nutshell points. Jerry will say, "And besides knocking on doors, there are *two* other ways I've found helpful in gaining new business."

> **Pro Pointer #27: Training a Big-Bertha
> pattern on your audience adds up to
> impact, impact, impact.**

In fact, if you're pressed for time or want to blast your main
point across, make a one-point big-gun speech.

> **Pro Pointer #28: A one-point big-gun
> speech can cause career-building
> detonations.**

The Lasso

Using a lasso pattern to catch your listeners' interest often
leads to an immensely successful talk. The trick lies in choosing an
absorbing lasso thread or theme to tie your talk together.
I think of the lasso pattern as looking like this:

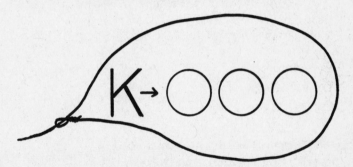

The "K" is your kick-off opener and the lasso the theme.
Here are a few ideas for lassos:
1. Thread of words can suggest a theme.   Martin Luther King,
Jr.'s speech with its recurring theme, "I have a dream," illustrates
a powerful lasso.
2. Enumerators. Giving a talk built around "six com-
mandments" . . . "profit points" . . . "grunts and grins" . . . and
similar techniques can make a fine audience lasso.
3. Literary. Recently a woman economist, speaking on
financial matters, planned her talk as if Benjamin Franklin had

written a letter home from Paris on today's inflation in the U.S. Her talk? Tremendous!

Sometimes, a speaker teeing off from "Alice in Wonderland" can mold an "Alice in Advertisingland" or "Alice in Fashionland" talk. Or he can paraphrase "The Greening of America" with "The Greening of the Convenience Store Industry." He talks about the greening of a good profit margin, the greening of a better-selling display, the greening of the addition of fashion items.

4. Novelty.   Perhaps a speaker will construct a talk around a letter from a kid at camp or look into the diary of a dweller in the 21st century. Or a speech planner, browsing in his newspaper for an idea, might come across an essay like this, "The Real Goodness of America," which columnist Sam Ragan ran in his column in the *Southern Pines Pilot.* Written by Kathy Power, a ninth-grader, it put her out front of 40,000 entrants in a national essay contest. Kathy word-painted:

> I walk down a street and I see doctors and lawyers playing in a sandbox.
> A scientist is patiently teaching her little brother, the president, how to ride a bicycle.
> While a mother wonders when she'll ever get her surgeon to cut his hair.
> And they are all free—to think and to choose, and they can work up to their dream.
> As I leave, a mother watches me and sees a dentist riding a skateboard down the street.

The prospective speaker might work out an adaptation of this for his talk. For a speech on how to service future customers in the automotive accessories business, a speaker might start off with a paraphrase like this:

> Tonight, let me take you on a walk in my neighborhood. We walk down a street and we see plumbers and marketing men playing marbles.

The speaker goes on to paraphrase the essay and then leads into his subject with a statement that these future plumbers, lawyers, etc., "will be our customers tomorrow—and they'll demand the best . . ."

So, now, breakfast, ponder, drink coffee, and choose the right pattern for your talk.

Setting Your Thought Computer for a "Wow" Opener

After you determine your pattern, look over your color-coded file cards and pick out one that's suitable for your opening gambit—this can range from an anecdote to a vivid statistic. If you need help for an opener, see Treasure Chest 1, the section beginning on page 143. This section offers actual openers and closers you can use as is or adapt. But picking out something nifty to *say* as an opener isn't enough. You want a *wow* opener.

Pro Pointer #29: Today, a wow opener usually means adding an arresting *visual*.

Often, this is a fairly *large* prop that will engage your audience's interest. Here are a few thought-starters about visuals.

Black photographer's bag.   Jerry, the contractor, might carry this to the platform and in his opener say while holding up the bag, "What do I use this bag for? To carry my money to the bank. You can, too, if you go after new pump and well customers three ways . . ."

Memo clothesline.   A manager opened her talk by unfurling a 6' rope to which she'd attached memos. She explained to her audience that she wrote this many suggestions for improvements before she received her first promotion. As she continued to write memos about profit-making ideas, she went up the ladder. She then gave tips for writing effective memos.

Jumbo ring.   A safety manager, asked to fill in for a no-show speaker, hurriedly borrowed a large ring from a member of the audience and rapidly walked up to the platform. He held up the ring and asked for a show of hands about how many of the foremen in the audience supervised workers who wore large rings or other jewelry. As a number of the foremen held up their hands, he pointed out that wearing jewelry could mean the loss of a finger or worse around machinery. He then went on to give safety tips.

Newspaper. A speaker, giving a seminar for real-estate salesmen, holds up a newspaper with a giant headline which he'd had set in special type and pasted in. (This is not expensive to do.) The headline reads: "Thousands Trying to Buy Homes." He points out that there is a *hidden* market of thousands of potential home buyers in the city. His seminar will help the salesmen identify and learn how to sell these hidden prospective home buyers.

As you read these ideas for visual props, I'm sure ideas for effective ones for your talk will pop into your mind. However, don't decide firmly on what you'll say or show for your opener. Hang loose in your thought till after lunch.

> **Pro Pointer #30: While you're doing your other work this morning, your mental computer may come up with something even more powerful.**

Reorganizing Your Cards

Now play a quick game of "organization" with your colored file cards. Lay them out behind your nutshell points and study them. Arrange them so each group of cards behind a point is in the *best* sequence.

Along about now you may find you've rapidly hit on a speech pattern, have a visually pow opener in mind, and your illustrative material arranged in the order you plan to use. But then, suddenly, speech-planning *jitters* may grab you. You wonder, even with all the above goodies, can you put together a stand-out talk? At this point, I like to sit at my desk and lay a bet with myself.

10 Ways to Jump Your Talk into Class A

Here's the way to judge whether you have a proper profit and loss sheet for your talk. "Profit and loss sheet?" you may say, coming awake. Yes, indeed. A profit and loss sheet can be most helpful.

So to put you on your speech-planning mettle, place a bet

with yourself *now*, whether you'll make a winner talk. If you make less than 110 points in the following quiz, you lose. Charge yourself 25¢ for each point made, and give the sum to charity. Should you make 110 points or more, you win. Pay yourself 25¢ for each point made and buy yourself a little gift.

While a good score is anything above 110, an *excellent* score falls in the 120-130 range. Jerry, for example, figures his speech profit and loss sheet at 123 points. Don't forget. If you end up paying yourself 25¢ for each point between 110-130, you can afford it. With a score that high, you'll make a Class A talk.

> **Pro Pointer #31: Once you start making Class A talks, they help your career (with raises and bonuses) move ahead.**

So, to help jump your talk into Class A, take this quiz and rate yourself:

1. Do I have plenty of stories—that is anecdotes, examples, jokes, one-liners, case histories? Give yourself five points for every story.
2. Do I have colorful quotes that help make my point? Note, the key word is *colorful*. Give yourself five points for each quote.
3. Have I rounded up several pertinent statistics? Again, five points for each statistic.
4. Do I have an intriguing *pattern* for my talk? Ten points.
5. Am I using nutshell points? If you're pure pro and make only *one* nutshell point, give yourself 15 points. If you make two main points, rate yourself 10. Three main points, score yourself five. And for each nutshell point over three you plan to use, charge yourself -5.
6. Will I use several references to important people? Business audiences like to hear about famous or authority figures. Allot yourself one point for each mention.
7. Have I come up with a visual grabber, like Jerry's patched jeans or the black photographer's bag? Award yourself 10 points if you use an interest-whetter visual in your opener.

8. Will I include several other visuals during my talk? Credit yourself with five points each.
9. Am I kicking-off with an arresting spoken statement or story? You are? This earns you 10 points.
10. Have I earmarked a smash closer? If you have, this rates five points.

This little game does one of two things:

1) You'll get a shot of confidence if you get a score between 120-130 points.
2) And if you don't, you can quickly picture where your talk is weak.

Then, during the day, you can think of ways to strengthen your talk. Sometimes it's as simple as adding more anecdotes and jokes to illustrate a nutshell point.

> **Pro Pointer #32: Now, as your business day starts, stay alert to illustrative material you run into that might beef up your talk.**

Steel-Trap Deciding on Your Opener and Closer

When you're back at your desk after lunch, make a steel-trap decision—one you won't alter—about exactly *what* anecdote, statement, visual effect, etc., you'll need for your wow opener. And ditto for your closer. Often, a pro closes his speech with a *bang!*

In picture-language, a problem/solution talk opener would end up looking like this:

A *bang* closer might be a summary of your important points, a specific call for action (such as urging your audience to write their congressmen), an effective story, or an inspiring quotation. You can add *bang* closers to any of the aforementioned patterns.

> **Pro Pointer #33: Once you make your opener/closer decision, never un-make it and substitute another opener/closer.**

The time spent in revamping an opener/closer could be used in polishing. And polishing puts the sparkle in your talk. So keep to your steel-trap decision.

Now, think about something else in your post-lunch speech session. Do you want to *write* out your talk? Let's be frank. There's nothing an audience loathes more than a speaker who hauls out a speech and reads it. If you want to give a spontaneous talk, scan the following tips on language that sinew a speech—but merely *familiarize* yourself with your material by studying your cards.

On the other hand, there are many times you must prepare a written talk in order to: (a) give someone a copy to review, (b) cite certain remarks precisely—perhaps for legal reasons, or (c) you lack time to rehearse adequately—necessary for a top-notch spontaneous talk.

Remember, many speakers write their talk to get a feeling of what they'll say—but give it off the cuff.

Crash-Course Drafting—Why Write too Much?

After 5:00 p.m. and your last rump session, grab a carton of milk or a Coke, take out your legal pad, and get ready to rapidly draft your talk. But before you start speed drafting, mentally say, "I won't write too much."

How do you streamline as you write?

> **Pro Pointer #34: Don't use a *lot of* words between your illustrations.**

Also plan to . . .

Use the High-Impact SWAP Formula. Keep in mind this simple formula for writing the kind of talk that massages your listeners' ears:

S hortening. Put *plenty* of speech shortening in your speech recipe. Short words, short sentences, short paragraphs, and short speech!

Wow opener.

A ction verbs, nouns, *few* adjectives and adverbs.

P unchy style. You get this by *end positioning*. Put the most important thought at the end of a sentence, paragraph, and section of speech.

Applying this high-impact SWAP formula can salvage a written talk, changing it from lavender-and-old-lace talk to lively.

Writing Like a Race-Car Driver

Now clear your desk, lay out your nutshell points with the cards arranged in the best order after each point. Review these for a few minutes to refresh your memory. Also think about your planned opener and closer. Then write like a race-car driver—*as fast as you can.*

In other words, don't write like you were riding a balky mule—scribble a few words then stop and ponder, cross out these words, choose another pen and write a few more words. Crumple up your sheet of paper and make a neat toss into an empty coffee cup.

Instead, remembering your overall plan—opener, nutshell points, illustrative examples, smash closer—write speedily and surely, as if you were racing in the big race. Don't stop to worry about grammar or choice of words. You can refine your prose later. If you can't think of a word, leave a blank and race on.

Why do I urge you to write like a manic race-car driver? Because then you'll (1) think and write better because you're writing spontaneously, and (2) you'll use a minimum of wordy connectors between your illustrative points.

> **Pro Pointer #35: The shorter the connectors between your illustrative material, the more your audience will relish your talk.**

Keeping the Seven-Tenths Proportion

Okay? Feel breathless? You should, if you wrote like a real race-car driver. Now grab your red magic marker. Quickly go through your draft and underline all the anecdotes, case histories, examples, jokes, and statistics.

Finished? Sit back and glance over the pages. Generally, you should see about seven-tenths of your words underlined in red. If you do, fabulous! If not, don't worry. Later I'll show you how to quickly increase your talk's red-cell count.

Turning Off with a Mini-Reward

As usual, you don't want to think about your talk when you go home this evening. You want to unwind. But since writing like a race-car driver gets the old adrenalin going, it's harder to turn off that imaginary spigot in your mind so you won't think about your talk.

On Night 4, I advise doing something *active* that gets you out of the house. In different surroundings and doing something engrossing, you tend not to mull over your talk. Bowling? A spy movie? A baseball game? Fine!

One of the best talk "turn-offers" I know is a speaker who has a hobby of train chasing. He'll go out on a lonely road, wait for a train, take aim, fire his flash camera, then race like crazy along country short-cut roads to another spot on the track. He'll catch the 40-mile-an-hour freight train several times in a 60-mile drive. Later he exchanges pictures and information with other train-chase hobbyists.

> Pro Pointer #36: He erases the blackboard of his speech thinking so that the next day he is fresh, fresh, fresh to work on his talk. You can, too.

In Control: Flagging Down Your Thought

Sometimes, the stimulus of an activity-filled evening means that when you get home, your thinking takes off again about your upcoming talk. Use the techniques mentioned in earlier chapters for turning off your thought.

Also, here's a sleep-coaxer speakers find helpful. Lace a cup of hot grapefruit juice with a teaspoon of strained honey. Dot with ½ teaspoon of butter. Sip slowly. This should quiet your thought tonight. And tomorrow you'll continue to forget your talk. In fact, you'll find tomorrow is "Funday"—working on your P.R. image.

Flashback

1. Choose a plan for your talk from four miracle patterns—(1) the striking story, (2) problem/solution, (3) the big gun, and (4) the lasso.
2. Program your thought for a nifty opener—from a striking statement to a joke.
3. Plus, turn your nifty opener into a wow opener with an arresting *visual* prop.
4. Quickly reorganize your color-coded file cards so they're in the best order to illustrate each nutshell point.
5. Make the steel-trap decision for your opener/closer. *Don't change your mind.*
6. How should you write your talk? Like a race-car driver—fast as you can. This will cause you to (a) think and write better and quicker, and (b) not put down boring phrases that act like steel wool in your listeners' ears.

How to Crash "Forget" Your High-Impact Talk —For Remarkable Results

Daily Step-Takers
- Forget your talk
- Draft a publicity announcement
- Polishing your publicity
- Plan how you'll look

Things You'll Need
- Yellow legal pad and ballpoint pen
- Background sheet folder
- Glossy picture of yourself

A favorite remark of Sam Ervin, Jr., the retired U.S. Senator who chaired the Watergate hearings, is: "If the good Lord had made us so that we could have hindsight in advance, a great many of our errors would be avoided."

In speech-making, the speaker always thinks of things he *should* have done to make his speech better. This chapter will help you have hindsight in advance.

Forget Your Talk in Your Desk Drawer

On Day 5, when you get into your office early, brimming with vitality from your previous activity-filled evening, it's hard to follow this next directive:

> Take a look at your speech folder. See that your speech, with numbered pages in proper order, is safely inside. Put it back in your desk drawer—without reading it!

> **Pro Pointer #37: Today, as you enjoy your portable breakfast at your desk, keep your talk in your desk drawer.**

Don't look at your talk the rest of the day. You want your subconscious computer to work on it while you're occupied otherwise. That way, you can quickly do dazzle editing tomorrow.

Forget Your Talk in Your Thinking

The real trick lies in abandoning your talk in your thinking. My friend Ken, a San Francisco exec, was a master at drafting a talk—then letting it lie in his desk drawer, neglected and unthought of, while he went skiing for a weekend. When he got back to town, he'd pick up his talk and quickly spot its weaknesses. With a little editing, he'd turn out a punchy, powerful talk.

> **Pro Pointer #38: Today, you must forget your talk.**

How? By turning to something else—drafting a publicity announcement of your talk.

Why You Need a Publicity Announcement

"But," you may say, "I don't want to draft a publicity announcement about my talk. All I want to do is put together a top talk—with no frills."

Today you *must* think about your public relations. A top

woman tennis pro commented that women tennis pros fall down on their job when they think their work ends when they stride off the court. She went on to point out that part of the job of women tennis stars is to handle their public relations well, give good interviews to the press, cordially sign autographs, make intelligent public comments on tennis when asked, and so on.

Business people, too, should handle their speech public relations correctly. And when giving a speech, this means preparing a pro-style publicity announcement.

Here are the simple steps you take in preparing your publicity release:

1. Prepare a one- or two-page publicity announcement. (In just a minute, you'll see how *easy* this is to draft.)
2. Ask the program chairman if he would like a copy of your release for reference.
3. If the program chairman says he doesn't know if *he'll* get around to sending out a release, volunteer to send the release to the media yourself.
4. Make a list of the media you'll distribute to—your industry newspaper; the media in the speech town, including newspapers, radio, and TV stations; a newsletter of your club; and your college alumni magazine. Your secretary can get addresses from your public library. *Send out your release widely!*

If you're with a large company and speaking on a business subject, ask the PR director if he wants to send a release on your speaking engagement. Should the PR director be clobbered with a rush job, the enterprising exec will volunteer to distribute his own PR release. He'll send a copy to the company house organ editor and the PR department for their files.

Why should you *bother* to send out photocopies of your publicity announcement so widely? You'll find throwing a publicity pebble into the media waters can have tremendous business value.

To illustrate, publicity about your speech may have these results:

• You may receive other invitations to speak.

- A business publication can write you to convert your talk into a by-line article.
- Newspaper, radio, and TV reporters may contact you for more *details* on an aspect of your talk. This can lead to a feature story.
- Good-quality job applicants may become interested in your company and send you a resume about their qualifications.
- People within your own company may become aware of your capabilities, which can result in your advancement.
- Key executives in other companies think about your potential. This can lead to job offers.
- Customers are occasionally reminded of your company's products—and place orders.
- Sometimes—if you're a principal in a company—someone gets in touch with you about buying into the company.
- You receive invitations to act as a consultant.
- A book publisher sometimes gets in touch with you to expand your expertise into a book.

As one PR expert puts it, "PR can sell anything from war to soap." You can't afford *not* to use its potential for personal growth.

> Pro Pointer #39: One secret of running up the ladder of success is not to make a quantity of talks, but quality talks, *and each publicized by releases.*

How a Contractor Drafts a Publicity Announcement

When Jerry drafts a publicity release, he uses a work sheet like the one shown here to easily pull together his basic information. You can, too.

Jerry photocopies the publicity work sheet and fills in his answers as shown at the bottom of page 75.

Publicity Work Sheet

1. Who, what, why, when, where:

2. Theme of talk:

3. About speaker's background:

4. Quote from talk:

5. Other meeting notes:

Publicity Work Sheet

1. Who, what, why, when, where: Jerry Bascomb will speak to the National Association of Contractors, Tuesday, January 25, 10:00 a.m., Grover Hotel, Las Vegas.

2. Theme of talk: "Attracting Profitable New Well and Pump Customers."

3. About speaker's background: President of Jerry Bascomb, Inc. Started highly profitable business three years ago.

4. Quote from talk: "My best business-getter is to knock on doors of new-home builders and ask for their well and pump business. I sell about 85% of people I contact."

5. Other meeting notes: Reservations chairman—Al Simmons, (phone number).

After filling out the publicity work sheet, Jerry knows what he wishes to say in his publicity release. So, he drafts the release.

Jerry Bascomb
President
Jerry Bascomb, Inc.
P.O. Box 399
Pacetown, N.C. (Zip)
(Phone number)
(Date)

News Release for Immediate Release

CONTRACTOR WILL TALK TO INDUSTRY GROUP

Jerry Bascomb, president of Jerry Bascomb, Inc., will speak to the National Association of Contractors, Tuesday, January 25, 10:00 a.m., at the Grover Hotel in Las Vegas.

"Attracting Profitable New Well and Pump Customers" is the theme of his talk.

Bascomb, who started his company three years ago, has designed his talk to show other contractors how to increase their business.

Reservations for the morning meeting can be made by calling Al Simmons, (phone number).

This is a minimum release. However, Jerry might decide to use a maximum release which would mean adding his quote and perhaps some details about special honors he has received. The advantage to the maximum release is that by giving the media more information, it often leads to more coverage.

So photocopy the Publicity Work Sheet, and as you sip your second cup of morning coffee sketch out your publicity release.

> **Pro Pointer #40: You'll be surprised at how *quickly* you can draft it.**

In fact, you'll have so much time before the rest of the office gang gets in, you can . . .

Look Over Your Background Sheet

With the creative work done this morning, put on your critic's hat and edit the introduction you did on Day 3. Here's how.

Shining It Up

Follow these tips for shining up your introduction:

1. Read through for general sense.
2. Any discordant notes? Mark "X" in margin and continue reading.
3. Go back and smooth out the discordant place(s).
4. Now read again carefully just for factual accuracies of dates, spelling of names, correctness of titles and locations, etc.
5. Give a third reading for slips of grammar, too-long sentences, etc. To spruce up grammar, simplify what you want to say, then restate. Bothered by a non-stop sentence? Chop it into two or three sentences.

Put a note on the Background Sheet for your secretary to type it on 8½" x 11" white bond paper.

Nifty Nit-picking

After you get back from lunch, and before you get into the afternoon's business nitty-gritty, get out the publicity release you prepared in the early morning hours. Do the same kind of editing and nit-picking you did on your introduction. Then, attach a note for your secretary to type it double-spaced on 8½" x 11" bond.

The Power of a Picture

Now, line up as many pictures of yourself as the number of publicity announcements you'll distribute.

Often, your public relations department has a suitable picture of you, and the negative will be on file with a photographer who can make copies in 24 hours. This black-and-white picture can be 8″ x 10″, 5″ x 7″, or even 3″ x 4″, with a *glossy* finish.

If you must start from scratch and get a picture made, call the photographer *without fail* now and make an appointment. Tell him your deadline.

Business people I've known have had extremely good luck phoning a reporter on a local paper. They'll ask the reporter for the name of a good head-shot photographer they can hire for a free-lance job. The reporter will finger the paper's ace head-shot photographer for you and you can call him.

> **Pro Pointer #41: A newspaper lensman can often drop by your office or home that day. He does good work, and many times his rates are far lower than those of studio portrait photographers.**

After you know the size of your picture (and the number you'll distribute), ask your secretary to type up, double-spaced on white bond sized to fit your photo, an identifying picture caption. Here's how a picture caption of Jerry, the contractor, would read:

```
                              Jerry Bascomb
                              President
                              Jerry Bascomb, Inc.
                              P.O. Box 399
                              Pacetown, N.C. (Zip)
                              Date

For Immediate Release
Jerry Bascomb, president of Jerry Bascomb, Inc.
```

Attach an identifying caption to the bottom of each of your pictures. Then fold the sheet over the face of the photograph to protect it from scratching. Also write your name *lightly* in a corner on the picture back, in case the caption gets detached in the newsroom.

And while your secretary is helping you get the picture show on the road, ask her to fit out 9″ × 12″ manila envelopes, each with two pieces of stiff cardboard backing. Use a red marker to mark each envelope: *First Class. Photo: Do Not Bend.* Then, when you get your photos, you can attach your release and mail or hand deliver it to the proper people. Send newspaper releases to "Business Editor" and radio and TV releases to "Program Director."

Pro Pointer #42: Make sure the media get their copies at least two days before the day of your speech.

Packaging Your Product

Sometime between 5:00 and 6:00 p.m., when the last head has poked in your door and said, "Hey, got a minute?" grab a soft drink or a candy bar. Sit, munch, and think for a few minutes about *how you'll look on the podium.* You know the old saying, "Two candidates of about equal ability apply for a job. The more personable one gets it." The more personable speaker reaps more speaking laurels.

Pro Pointer #43: Packaging yourself has never been more vital than when making a talk.

You must dress and groom yourself appropriately; you must choose the right colors and style for podium appeal; and you must project the image you want.

Here are some pointers to help you package yourself:

Overall appearance. Your overall grooming should be impeccable—including clean, pressed clothes, manicured nails, shined shoes.

Hair. Whether you wear a conventional business cut or perhaps a longer look (if you're in the advertising or artistic world), go to an ace hair stylist (possibly *not* your family barber) and get your hair washed, styled, and blown dry.

I advise going to an expert hair stylist because you want to make sure your hair style is not out of date. You can always wear an "adaption" of a current style. When you're speaking about current problems and wearing yesterday's hair style, your audience wonders how credible you are.

Clothes. "Appropriate" is the key word for your clothes when you make a talk. If you speak at an informal seminar, dress informally—a good quality leisure suit or sports outfit. If you make a talk to business people in a business setting, wear a *good* version of your everyday business clothes. Women should remember that a pant suit can hide leg trembling. For men a bright tie and for women a bright outfit is desirable on the speaker's platform, since bright colors attract and hold the listeners' eyes.

It will pay to get professional help in choosing what you'll wear. If you know an excellent haberdasher—and even it you're only picking up a new tie for your speaking occasion—consult him. Tell him the setting and purpose of your talk and what you plan to wear. Ask him if this is correct. An expert's opinion can make a tremendous difference. He might advise you to wear a color combination of shirt and tie you hadn't thought of, for a very "right" effect from the platform.

A woman speaker—even if she's only going to buy a new scarf for her speaking occasion—can discuss the suitability of her outfit with a knowledgeable boutique saleswoman. The speaker will get the *latest* and *best* thinking.

Pro Pointer #44: Women speakers (and men, too) can seek the advice of a free-lance wardrobe consultant (usually a woman).

You can often get the name of a free-lance fashion consultant by phoning the fashion editor of your local newspaper. The wardrobe consultant will drop by your house and suggest from *your present wardrobe* an effective combination for the platform. Or, if you wish, she'll also suggest a new piece or two you might add. She often charges from $15 to $35 an hour and usually a consultation for a speaking date doesn't take more than one or two hours.

> **Pro Pointer #45:** A wardrobe consultant can help you take the "waste" of time and money out of assembling your platform look. And you'll have a standout look you can use for *several more speaking engagements.*

In Control: How Your "I-Don't-Care" Attitude Can Strengthen Your Talk

Do you recall times in your life when you prepared for something, did it by the book, and improved somewhat? And then at some point you said, "Oh, the heck with it. I don't care," and then casually did the thing—*and did it tremendously well!*

For example, perhaps you've taken golf lessons from a golf pro and improved your game somewhat. But one day, without really trying, you step up and swing at a ball—and make a great shot. And with that same "I-don't-care" attitude, you continue to do far better all the way around the course.

After working to improve yourself in a business skill, there's nothing like developing an "I-don't-care" attitude in your leisure hours. It helps you take giant strides towards your objective.

So tonight, fan your "I-don't-care" attitude about your upcoming talk by relaxing completely. Don't think about your talk at all. And remember, in order not to think about your talk, substitute some absorbing mental activity—bridge, chess, a gripping TV show. If you can truly click off your speech thinking tonight, you'll be fresh to shape-up a big-league talk tomorrow.

Flashback

1. On Day 5, cool off your talk by letting it stay *in* your desk drawer and *out* of your thinking.
2. Make a photocopy of the Publicity Work Sheet and fill in the answers.
3. Use this information to painlessly draft a publicity announcement.
4. Arrange for a *glossy*-finish picture of yourself to send with each publicity release.

5. Plan your personal packaging—what you'll wear, how you'll look.
6. The Miracle Speech Power method suggests consulting a peanuts-priced wardrobe consultant who'll save you time and money and help you look like a million on the platform.

How to Power Shape
Your Entire Talk
—From Zingy Opening
to Punchy Closing

Daily Step-Takers
- Product control; inspection of anecdotes, statistics and quotes
- Estimate speech length
- Memorizing head and feet
- Crash checking on your speech setting

Things You'll Need
- Your talk manuscript
- Yellow legal pad
- Ballpoint pen
- Red and green felt-tip pens

Years ago, Catherine the Great of Russia faced a problem that bothers speech pruners. Her friend, Denis Diderot, a scholar,

urged Catherine to change her form of government by simply
renouncing the old form. At this advice, Catherine frowned,
pondered, and finally said:

> These fine-sounding principles of yours may be all very well
> in the world of books, but they do not suit the world of af-
> fairs. You do your work on patient paper. I, who am only an
> empress, have to work on human skins and they are ticklish.

You'll shortly give a talk. And handling your listeners is
ticklish business.

> **Pro Pointer #46: That's why on Day 6,
> you'll go through your talk for *product
> control* so you won't tickle your audience
> the wrong way.**

Product Control

Someone once defined product control as "The controls
necessary to keep the product quality at a desired level." This
definition fits the product control of your talk. What is the desired
product level for your speech? Catherine Drinker Bowen, a best-
selling biographer, once said that she kept a small sign above her
desk. Whenever she glanced up from her work, she read the words,
"Will the reader turn the page?"

> **Pro Pointer #47: The desired product level
> for your talk is to keep the listener so
> *interested* he turns the pages—that is, he
> stays tuned in during the 15 minutes or so
> you'll speak.**

The tips given below will help keep him tuned in. Once you
follow these tips—and they're easy—you'll begin to feel wonder-
fully confident about your upcoming talk.

Read Through with Your "Gut-Feeling" Glasses

As you sip your morning coffee, get ready to look *closely* at
the talk you drafted on Day 4.

How closely will you look? When speakers ask me that question, I like to tell them about the "lemon experiment" in the art classes at the University of Northern Iowa.

On a Monday morning each student picks out a lemon from a shopping bag. He's told to "live" with his lemon day and night—carry it, look at it, study it, run his fingers over it, sniff it, but *not* mark it any way. On Wednesday, the students are suddenly directed to drop their lemon into a shopping bag. Then each student is asked to pick out *his* lemon. Almost always, each student recognizes *his* lemon!

In the next few minutes, you're going to recognize every facet of your talk—and polish it.

So, now, mentally put on your "gut-feeling" glasses and read your talk through for the general effect. While you read, mentally slip into the skin of one of your potential listeners. As you read, don't worry about fly specks—an awkward sentence, a fuzzy anecdote, a too-sudden transition—but simply read your talk to see if you've written a page turner . . . if people will find what they're hearing *absorbing*.

If you finish reading through, and feel you scored with a keep-'em-listening talk—though it needs polishing—great. You'll enjoy sprucing it up. On the other hand, if you feel the talk will hardly keep your listeners out of the land of Nod, look it over carefully for colored lines. Remember, on Day 4 you underlined in red all the anecdotes, examples, jokes, one-liners, statistics, quotes from authorities, mini-case histories? Does seven-tenths of your talk show up underlined in red, as recommended on Day 4?

> **Pro Pointer #48: In many cases, once this proportion is adjusted you transform a talk from soggy to super.**

The editing pointers below will help you attain the seven-tenths proportion. These pointers will help you put a shine on your talk that'll put a shine on your listeners' faces.

Make "I, S, F" Marginal Notes

While you enjoy a second cup of coffee, again, mentally dressed in the skin of a listener, read your talk through. Mark "I" (for illustration) by any passage over 75 words that does not show any red underlining.

Next, be alert for any passage that seems to move "slowly"— that is, seems boring, wordy, or confusing. Use your red marker to mark "S" in the margin by this passage. Plan to cut and condense.

What if you come to an interesting point in your talk, but find it goes by too rapidly—too telegraphically? Your gut feeling tells you this section goes by so fast you'll hit your reader in his puzzlement zone. He won't grasp what you mean. Mark "F" in green in the margin to indicate you'll need to slow this passage down by adding more details.

Adjust the sections you've marked.

Zip Through with Your Anecdote-Appraisal Glasses

When Kipling, the great British writer, was a young man, he wrote some poetry that pleased him. Later he showed the poems to his mother, a well-known poet. She criticized her son's poems rather severely. And Kipling felt hurt. His mother pointed out that there's no mother in poetry. And there can be no mother in looking at your anecdotes.

> **Pro Pointer #49: You must judge your anecdotes as your worst enemy would judge them.**

So with your anecdote-appraisal glasses on, read through just your stories—including examples, mini-case histories, jokes, etc. Here are a few things to ask yourself about a story. Is it . . .

- Appropriate? Does this story make the point I want to make?
- Effective? Is it told as effectively as I can tell it? Often, you can shorten or simplify an anecdote to give it more punch.
- Short? Today's audiences like their anecdotes quick. Perhaps you should substitute three one-liners for a one-minute joke. To get more sparkling stories and witty words, use the handy source section in Treasure Chest 2 of this book.

- Nonhurtful? Will this story step on the toes of anyone in my audience? Don't risk turning off any of your listeners with a religious, ethnic, or tasteless sex story. Let your anecdotes be deliciously interesting, amusing, and . . . *kindly*.
- Personalized? Where possible, have I personalized an anecdote? In telling it, do I use the names of a couple of people in my audience? (Always check with them in advance to be sure this is okay.)

> **Pro Pointer #50: Personalizing stories and examples with actual names of audience members, audience problems, giving the audience's industry as a setting, etc., gives your stories *tremendous audience appeal*.**

Fix up any stories that need it. Then remove your anecdote-appraisal glasses and . . .

Shift into Your Statistical Glasses for a Run-Through

On this reading, only look at your statistics. As we mentioned earlier, you generally don't want too many statistics in your talk. A few statistics, fitly chosen and spoken, can pep up your talk. Here are pointers in judging figures:

Different approach. Sometimes you can present your statistics in a fresh way. Example: Talking about the state of the nation, a speaker doesn't say "Seven percent of Americans are unemployed." Instead, he uses a *different* approach and concludes his talk with, "God Bless America . . . 93% of Americans are employed."

Proof. Sometimes a statistic can be used effectively to prove your point. Example: A speaker, wishing to prove that a business person with a photographic hobby was successful, said, "After writing, taking photographs, and publishing a pictorial historical guide to her city, she netted over $100,000."

O. O. E.'s. One's own experiences can often make compelling statistics. Example: Jerry, the contractor, needs a striking statistic to point out how knocking on doors works well in gaining new customers. Not having one ready-made, how does he find such a statistic? He compiles it himself. He looks over his records and counts his calls and signed contracts. The result? He comes up with the statistic that he closes 85% of his calls—a fascinating statistic to listeners thinking of adding this service to their business.

Revamp any statistic that needs it. Next, since you want to get the most chips on the table for the success of your talk, slip off your statistical glasses and . . .

Slip on Your Quirky Glasses and Look at the Quotes

Read through your quotes from authorities and see if any of these tips apply:

Paraphrase.   Do you have a long stretch of comment by an authority? Pick up the pace of your talk by briefly paraphrasing long comments.

Juicy.   Do include juicy, ear-grabbing quotes. For example, Jerry, wishing to emphasize certain factors in achieving success, finds he has used the following quotes from a daily newspaper story about a woman who, with her husband, started a thriving chain of figure salons. In one quote she says:

"I come from very basic origins."

In the other quote she says:

"Sometimes education can teach you to be too deliberate.
The secret of success is to leap and then work your way out!"

He discards the first quote and keeps the juicy second quote. Just as the doctor buries his mistakes (so goes the old joke), you can cut out your weak quotes.

> **Pro Pointer #51: Then, when you give your talk, you come up with nothing but lively quotes, so your talk sounds lustrous.**

Composite. Sometimes in scanning your quotes, you find you need more. What do you do? Make up a composite quote. That is, make up conversational remarks that *could* have been said.

For example, Jerry wishes to bring out the fact that his advertising paid off. He's used a statistic to show this but he'd also like quotes to drive home the point. Unfortunately, he never saved any letters from customers or noted their comments. So, from memory, Jerry jots down the following remarks:

- One man phoned me and said, "Your ad said you'll dig wherever you can get a rig in. Can you dig a well up the side of the mountain?"
- Another man said, "I heard your ad on the radio this morning. Your firm's just what I'm looking for."
- "I was browsing through the Yellow Pages and I saw your ad," wrote one lady. "Does your firm service out-of-county customers?"

These sprightly quotes indicate to the listener that advertising pays. And they're more lively to listen to than a remark such as, "Our ads draw responses from a number of people."

As soon as you get your illustrative material squared away, think about the advice one of the country's most popular speakers always gives his listeners, "To be successful, you must have a love affair with your job."

So, sip some more coffee, and prepare to do an editing chore that I always think of as "having a love affair with your job." Because right now, your job is to prepare a good talk. By *loving* the next steps you'll find you take them easily and deftly.

Ten Guides for a Vital Talk

Applying the hints in the ten guides below puts the final bloom on your talk. So now go through it and make it *bloom*.

1. Length. In judging the length of your talk manuscript, figure that you'll start with audience compliments and ice-breakers. We'll talk about these on a later day. As you give your talk you'll add body language and visual aids. All of this takes time.

On this basis, you can estimate you'll talk about 100 words a minute. For a 15-minute talk, you'll need about 1500 words. So count your words. Need to cut? It's often easiest to cut a talk by dropping an illustration or two. Next, roughly adjust your talk length, with scissors and tape.

If the talk is only a couple of minutes short, leave it that way. But if you need to build it up, add a few illustrations.

2. Conversational. As one wit said, "A speech is not an essay on hind legs." Examine your talk to see if it's conversational. Use shirt-sleeve language.

3. Markers. Check to make sure your talk doesn't sound like a river of words flowing out. Put in plenty of markers—words like "my first point" ... "my second point" ... etc. See the "building bridges" section on page 149 of this book for suggestions about this.

4. Repetition. Note if you have a strong phrase you might use several times to make your point. Experts have found that you must say something five times for an audience to get it completely.

5. Vivid verbs. On Day 4 I alerted you to write with action verbs. Now read through and see if you generally use dove-gray or colorful verbs. For example, Jerry might find he wrote: "The first day I *contacted* 10 new-home builders." He scrutinizes the verb "contacted" and decides it's as dove-gray as they come. So he crosses out "contacted" and writes, "The first day I *pounded* on the doors of 10 new-home builders." Notice how a listener will start to sit up with a colorful verb.

Pro Pointer #52: You can enliven a talk by coloring dove-gray verbs vivid.

One trick for making verbs vigorous: As you cast about for a zippy verb when you edit, make a fist with your non-writing hand. Punch the air as if you were boxing when you read the sentence through. Often, an *alive* verb will pop off the end of your pen.

6. Striking out adjectives and adverbs. Again, as we mentioned on Day 4, you often need to get rid of unnecessary adjectives and adverbs. If you do use an adjective, try to use one that's fresh and vigorous. For example, Jerry finds these sentences:

Here's an added benefit to pounding on doors for business. You frequently find yourself also enjoying the great wonderful natural beauties of the outdoors.

First, Jerry scans for adverbs. He knocks out "frequently" and "also." Then he says to himself, "I've heard that phrase 'natural beauties of the outdoors' about a million times. Will these words grab my audience?" He shakes his head. He reshapes the passage. It now reads:

One added benefit: When I'm pounding on doors, I watch clouds playing tag, birds high-diving, cats wrestling—nature's Wide World of Sports.

In reshaping, ask yourself: How do I really feel about the way I put this? Is this part numbing or neat? You may find yourself writing something else—something that will make your audience say, "Gee, this guy's *fun* to listen to."

7. Negatives/positives. Scamper through your talk once more and consider the negatives and positives. In most cases, it's better to touch on negatives and focus on positives. So make adjustments where necessary.

8. Too much detail. A speaking expert said it well, "The secret of being boring is to tell everything." As you go through your talk, cut out too much unnecessary detail. When you shrink unneeded detail, you *increase* the power and punch of your talk.

9. Buzz words. Call out industry buzz talk. Let's say you're an insurance man and speaking about ' nonforfeiture value" . . . "settlement options" . . . "whereas" . . . "hereinafters." Switch to words you'd use with smart ten-year-olds.

> **Pro Pointer #53: Write your talk so the college football star can understand it. Let the college president look out for himself.**

On the other hand, audiences love it when you knead picturesque expressions into your talk. For instance, they are delighted when Ford Motor Company president Lee Iacocca comes out with "brushfire inflation."

10. Alliteration/rhyme. John Kennedy, 35th president of the United States, added rhyme and alliteration to his speeches to help make his points memorable.

You can, too. As you know, alliteration is the use of words beginning with the same letter. Jerry might spot a phrase, "business help." in his talk and give it more pizazz with the alliteration, "business booster."

Next step: Go through your manuscript, reading aloud to yourself. Make two slashes after each complete phrase you'd read on a one breath exhalation. For instance, Jerry's manuscript might have slashes like this:

> I've found you can attract//profitable new well and pump customers three ways://First, by pounding on doors;//second, by pleasing present customers;//and third, by advertising.//

Put a note on your manuscript and ask your secretary to type it on 5″ × 8″ cards, in CAPS, triple-spaced, with one slash-marked phrase to a line.

One of Jerry's talk cards would look like the Line-Typed Card shown here.

```
I'VE FOUND YOU CAN ATTRACT

PROFITABLE NEW WELL AND PUMP CUSTOMERS THREE WAYS

FIRST, BY POUNDING ON DOORS

SECOND, BY PLEASING PRESENT CUSTOMERS

AND THIRD, BY ADVERTISING.
```

Arranging for a Fast Tour

After lunch, before you get into the afternoon's activities, pick up your phone. Call the program chairman and arrange for a fast tour of the talk premises at the end of the day. If your talk is out of town, phone the program chairman and arrange to inspect the speech premises several hours beforehand. Ask any "premise" questions that come to mind.

Next, get out your talk once more. Now you're about to begin a small task that adds *huge benefits* to your talk's success.

Memorizing the Head and Feet

One speech coach gives this recipe for a speech: "Start with a boom; build up to an earthquake."

Today we'll concentrate on the boom. That's your opener. Take your opener and rechristen it. The ancients liked to compare the parts of the talk with the human body—the beginning, the head; middle, the torso; ending, the feet. From now on you'll find your talk shaping up better if you think of your opening statement as the head of your talk. Take the head *and memorize it*. Also *memorize the feet* of your talk.

For example, Jerry might memorize word for word the problem/solution head mentioned earlier. Jerry would also memorize word for word the following feet of his talk:

> In closing, remember, if I've told you about getting new business, you've heard me . . .
> If I've showed you, you understand . . .
> If you do it, it's yours!

So whether you give your talk extemporaneously or read it, commit the head and feet to memory.

> **Pro Pointer #54: Memorizing the head and feet keeps you from making opener and closer goofs that spoil your speech.**

As you have odd bits of time from now till you give your talk, spend them memorizing the head and feet.

Four Crash Checks on Your Speech Setting

At the end of your day, drop by at the place where you'll give your talk and quickly check out these details:

√ **Introduce yourself** to the room's engineer.

> **Pro Pointer #55: Make a note of the engineer's name. Then, during your presentation, if necessary, you can efficiently say, "Carl, could you open a window?" or "Carl, could we have the slide screen a little higher?"**

√ **Discuss any problems** you might run into with the mike and lectern (or podium). Do you know how to handle that type of mike? Remember, if the mike swivels, have it bend towards you. If you bend towards it, you will ruin how you look.

Try the lectern (or podium) for height. Try not to talk at one higher or lower than about the bottom of your breast pocket. If you're short, ask for a riser (platform) to stand on. If you're tall, can the engineer lift the lectern with a wood wedge? If you need them, will he have a blackboard, eraser, and chalk? Will he provide a table for your props? Mention anything you might need.

√ **Seating.** A large auditorium and you expect only a fairly small group? Ask if the program chairman has requested the engineer to rope off a section in the front so the audience won't scatter around the auditorium. If the chairs are movable, perhaps you can suggest a better arrangement for them to the program chairman. Perhaps a semicircle around the speaker?

> **Pro Pointer #56: The *closer* the speaker is to his listeners, the better.**

√ **Lighting.** Notice the available light. Will it be sufficient for you to read your talk? Will it be comfortable for the audience and yourself? Talk over with the engineer whether the light should be increased or dimmed during your presentation.

If you're a woman, check your makeup under the available lighting. If you appear washed out or see shadows on your face, ask the engineer for three-quarters lighting.

Relax, Relax, Relax

After viewing your speech setting, and with your speech edited and put in for typing, go home, enjoy a good dinner, and *relax*.

In Control: Two "Pills" for a Strong Speech

On Day 6, after editing, often comes the big test: Can you keep your thoughts from swinging back to today's speech work? ("Maybe I should have edited that anecdote another way." "Maybe I should substitute another statistic.") Or maybe your thoughts swing towards tomorrow—things you should do about your talk. Such mental stewing is profitless. So take two "pills" to tranquilize your thoughts.

De-tense by taking a short walk. A change of scene will help break up any fretting thought pattern. Also, as you walk, take shallow, slow, steady breaths that fill your lungs *horizontally* instead of vertically. Such breathing helps you unkink.

The dog-and-stick pill. Did you ever watch a dog chase a stick his master throws? What happens if the stick falls, say, into a pond? Does the dog sit down and think, "Heck, I'm a failure as a dog. I should have run faster and caught that stick? Now I'll never be able to retrieve it. No telling what'll happen because I didn't do a good job on that stick." No, the dog doesn't beat up on himself with that kind of thinking. He just comes back to his master and waits for him to throw another stick, and then chases it with zest. No worrying is involved.

If you want to come out slugging tomorrow on your talk, just say to yourself, "Maybe I didn't edit everything perfectly. But I did the best I could today. Actually, I retrieved quite a few sticks. And if I do the right things tomorrow, I'll be okay." And you will.

Gulping these mental pills will help you relax tonight. That way on Day 7, you can wake up fresh and begin the exciting and miracle method of becoming a high-impact performer.

Flashback

1. Read through with your "gut-feeling" glasses.
2. Mark "I" where you need more illustrations; "S" for slow passages you should cut; "F" for too-fast sections where you need to add more details.

3. Next, check if anecdotes are appropriate? Short? Personalized? Adjust where needed.
4. Are your statistics striking? Presented in a different manner? Specially tailored out of your own experience?
5. Slip on your quirky glasses and look at quotes from authorities. Should you briefly paraphrase some? Are they juicy? Eliminate dull ones.
6. Including time for compliments to the audience, using visual aids and body language, figure about 1500 words for a 15-minute talk.
7. *Memorizing* the head and feet is goof-proof insurance.
8. Check out your speech setting—mike, lectern, lighting, prop table, etc.
9. De-tense in the evening by gulping take-a-stroll and dog-and-stick "pills."

How to Emerge Almost Miraculously As a Vital Performer

Daily Step-Takers
- Work out several times today by reading or delivering your talk extemporaneously
- Achieve eye-power
- Weave in visual aids
- Shadow-box with body English

Things You'll Need
- 5" X 8" file cards
- Black, green, and red felt-tip pens
- Photocopied critique sheet
- Alarm clock or timer

As you slip into your office on Day 7, open the blinds and put down your portable breakfast, suddenly, it hits you that "the speech" lies only three days away. Here's a statement to think about.

A prominent New York speechwriter/coach maintains: "If a speaker is willing to spend more than three hours in rehearsal workouts, he can be spectacular."

This prediction is true. Let me repeat it:

> If a speaker is willing to spend more than three hours in rehearsal workouts, he can be spectacular.

That's it. That's one of the big secrets of success in talking. Let me tell you this once again:

> *If a speaker is willing to spend more than three hours in rehearsal workouts, he can be spectacular.*

So take a swallow of coffee and let's take the first step toward turning your talk into a *red-hot speech*.

Warm Up by Repeating the Memorized Head and Feet

Thomas Edison said something that applies to rehearsing. He advised, "Everything comes to him who hustles while he waits."

You'll recall that yesterday you started to memorize the head and feet of your talk. Now, on Day 7, as you eat breakfast, *hustle.* Stand up, and as you drink your coffee say the *memorized* head and feet of your talk. As you talk, look around your office, at a chair, an ashtray, a book—as if they were people you were talking to. And during the day, when you're driving or waiting for a meeting to start, say the head and feet to yourself till you have them down cold.

Pro Pointer #57: You must work on your talk till you can repeat the head and feet *word perfect* ... at the snap of your fingers ... anytime ... anyplace.

Why is it so necessary to know the head and feet from memory? The ability to have them *indelibly* stamped on your mind means that in these two vital spots of your talk: (1) you sell yourself to your audience by looking directly at them, (2) you don't jumble a thought sequence or grope for words, and (3) you say the words in a planned, punchy order.

One thing more that testifies to the importance of this memory trick: Business people spend big bucks to learn tips like this in exclusive executive speaking programs.

Pro Pointer #58: Memorizing the head and feet is a simple way to help turn your talk from dull to dynamic.

Work Out by Reading Your Speech Aloud

If you plan to "read" your speech, here's how I mentally picture the parts of the talk:

$$M \cdots RT \cdots M$$

The first "M" stands for the memorized head; the "RT" for the "read" torso, including the steering sentence; and the second "M" for the memorized head.

So now, if you have opted to read your talk, get out your 5″ × 8″ cards. Here's how to proceed in a rehearsal workout for a "read" talk:

1. You'll say your memorized head and feet, looking around at objects in your office as if you were locking eyes with your listeners.

2. You'll read the torso of your talk from your cards with the line-grabber technique. This means: simply drop your eyes (try not to bend your head) to your card, grab a line with your eyes, raise your gaze, and say the line *directly to the audience*.

Pro Pointer #59: Don't split a line—that is, say part of it, drop your eyes, pick up the rest of the line, and say that to your listeners.

As you continue to practice the line-grabber technique and *familiarize* yourself with your material, you can take in several lines at a glance and say *them* from recall as you look out at your audience.

> **Pro Pointer #60: Your final goal will be to look at your audience *80%* of the time.**

3. You'll use body language—such as facial expressions, gestures, movements of your entire body. You'll also use your visual aids—make-shift ones if your planned ones aren't ready.

4. You'll repeat your memorized ending, using eye contact with your audience.

How to Talk Off the Cuff

As two moths flitted lackadaisically around a closet containing a man's and woman's formal evening clothes, one said to the other, "I hate these formal dinners."

Audiences may like formal affairs—but they abhor a *boringly* read speech. (Though, if planned, rehearsed, and talk/read as Miracle Speech Power teaches, your "read" talk can be spectacular—and you come off a hero!) However, when a speaker stands up and indicates he'll talk *off the cuff,* his listeners feel a thrill of interest. They say to themselves, "This fellow looks like he may be dynamic!" But then their thrill of interest turns into wariness. They worry that the talker without a script may turn out to be one of the following three types of off-the-cuff speakers they've heard too often:

- *The Rambling Wreck.* He's the off-the-cuff talker who's jotted a few lines on a scrap of paper, never rehearsed, and stands up and rambles on and on. He makes no particular point and often rambles his career into the ground.
- *The Thought Un-Collector.* He arises and apologizes, "I haven't had much chance to collect my thoughts on this subject." In the next few minutes, he demonstrates he's spoken truthfully. As the Great Vacuum Speaker chug-chug-chugs along, he drives his audience into fantasyland.

- *The Er-Ah-Um Artist.* After confessing to his listeners, "I'm no speaker," he proves it. And he also shows he's a serious contender for the Guiness World Championship for er-ah-ums, key rattling, and nervous shifting.

So, knowing that the audience is hoping you won't turn out to be one of these off-the-cuff flops, here's how to work out to make your extemporaneous speech snazzy . . . and the evening all-the-way wonderful for your audience.

On Day 7, begin familiarizing yourself with your talk so you can give it smoothly . . . and excitingly. Here's the way I mentally see the parts of the extemporaneous talk.

M ⋯ ET ⋯ M

The first "M" stands for the memorized head; the "ET" for the extemporaneous torso, including the steering sentence; and the second "M" for the memorized feet.

In rehearsing your off-the-cuff talk, keep these steps in mind:

1. You'll start by saying the head from memory.
2. You'll give the torso of your talk with your decided-upon steering sentence, nutshell points, and illustrative material. But you'll speak the torso in *fresh* words each time. You won't memorize the torso.
3. You'll end with the memorized feet of your talk.

Whether you read your talk or say it off the cuff, talk *conversationally.* One way to achieve a conversational attitude is to think: (a) you're not up before an audience talking *down* to them, (b) you're not talking *up* to an audience, (c) but you're on a *level* with your audience. You should feel almost as if you're discussing something on an informal one-to-one basis.

Business and professional people tend to become *stiff,* even pompous-sounding, in front of an audience. To de-stiffen your talk, one trick is to stop rehearsing it. Then, as if to a friend, describe, for a couple of minutes, a favorite trip you've taken or a phase of your pet hobby. Notice the enthusiastic, conversational way you talk. When you resume your rehearsal, speak that same way, whether you read or give your speech extemporaneously.

Why You Must Follow the Crash Five-Minute Break

Reading your talk or giving it off the cuff takes concentration. So set your alarm clock or timer. At the end of each run-through (if your talk's no longer than 15 minutes), or at the end of 10 minutes (if it's a 20-minute talk), take a five-minute break. Stop rehearsing and do something different. Have a bite of Danish. Get a coffee refill. Glance at a memo on your desk. Then, resume your practice.

> **Pro Pointer #61:** A five-minute break after 10 or 15 minutes will let you perform *far better* than if you dig in and keep rehearsing nonstop.

Marking Your Talk Cards

After you find yourself more familiar with the speech you'll be reading, mark your cards for emphasis and volume. The Symbols Chart provides symbols you might use.

See the Marked Card which shows how Jerry marks up one of his 5″ x 8″ talk cards.

Now, as you continue to rehearse your "read" talk, follow your emphasis and volume markings to get a varied effect. And if you're rehearsing an extemporaneous talk, begin to add the preceding techniques to it. For example, say some parts louder, some softer, as appropriate . . . pause for emphasis and effect . . . "color" a word to make it sound more exciting.

What if you note that you're speaking a lot of er-ah-ums? Stop when you do this and think, *without saying anything,* about what you wish to say. Then go on. This tip will weed out many of the clutter words. If necessary, follow this tip in your actual talk.

> **Pro Pointer #62:** An audience likes to see a speaker's face when he's *thinking,* not talking, and it gives your listeners time to think about points you've made.

Symbols Chart

- Underline a word once for emphasis like <u>this.</u>
- Underline a word twice for more emphasis like <u>this</u>.
- Put a slash like this **/** for a slight pause.
- Add two slashes like this **//** for a greater pause.
- To gradually decrease volume use this mark: **>**
- Want to gradually increase volume? Draw this: **<**
- To remind yourself to slow down a passage, bracket it in red. **[ ]**
- Want to speed it up? Bracket it in green.
- When you want to lower your voice, draw a down arrow. **↓**
- Point the arrow up when you wish an upward inflection. **↑**
- To pronounce a word with feeling, circle it. For example: Circling (delicious) nudges you to say it so it sounds tasty.

I'VE FOUND YOU CAN ATTRACT

<u>PROFITABLE</u> NEW WELL AND PUMP CUSTOMERS <u>THREE</u> WAYS

<u>FIRST,</u> //BY POUNDING ON DOORS //

<u>SECOND</u>,//BY (PLEASING) PRESENT CUSTOMERS //

AND <u>THIRD,</u> //BY ADVERTISING.

Five Aids to Eye-Power

Here are checkpoints to help you achieve strong eye-contact:

√ In eye-contacting your audience, *variety* is the name of the game.

√ Keep moving your eyes around, hitting a different person in a different section of the room each time. Note the figure which follows: It shows how Jerry might direct his eyes when using eye-power. Hint: Touch your fingertip on each number in sequence and you'll see the movement of the eyes more clearly.

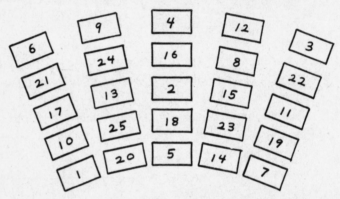

√ When using eye-contact, look directly *into* the person's eyes. One speech consultant calls this "eye-dropping" . . . as if using an eye-dropper and dropping a sentence or two into each person's eyes.

√ Don't linger too long with one listener. On the other hand, be deliberate enough to say a sentence or two to the same person.

> **Pro Pointer #63:** If you feel a bit inhibited about gazing into your listeners' eyes, look longer into the *friendly* eyes—but not too long. You'll soon feel relaxed.

√ *Organized* eye-contact. Occasionally, people have a severe problem looking into their listeners' eyes. If *you* have this problem, *organized* eye-contact can help you.

For example, if Jerry employs organized eye-power, here's the orderly way his eyes move.

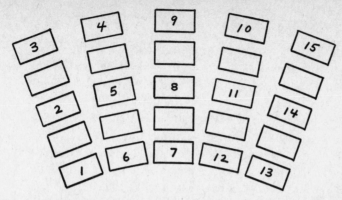

After he finished all the rows, Jerry starts again in the left section, but hits different people's eyes as he moves back in the row.

> **Pro Pointer #64:** Your audience won't get restive under such organized eye-contact. Instead, you'll rivet their interest.

"But," you may say, "aren't all these tricks really Mickey Mouse?" "Mickey Mouse, yes, but it's Mickey Mouse that works," I answer. In fact, it works so well that, again, executive speech coaches charge hundreds of dollars for a few coaching sessions of such tricks. So, avail yourself of these tested tips that help turn a talk from stodgy to sparkling . . . and help jump a career from a valley to a mountain top.

Weaving in Visual Aids

One pro speaker likes to say:

> Building confidence is done with *facts*.
> Building a good speech is done with *acts*.

Today, achieving a supertalk in business is done with *acts*—visual aids. From now on, as you rehearse, use whatever visual aids you have ready—or use *substitutes*. Tomorrow, I'll give you a few tricks for handling your visual aids with major-league speaker's clout.

Shadow-Boxing with Body English

Perhaps when you started out this morning, as the pink was fading out of the sky and you were faced with your rehearsal workouts, you thought about the old Spanish proverb, "I don't want the cheese, I just want to get out of the trap."

Yet, as you see, the workout trap is fun, and by now, you may be anticipating the cheese—the accolades and career rewards— that comes from delivering a smashing speech. Believe me, there's nothing like that kind of cheese. So now, let's not stop to let our mouths water but let's get closer to the cheese.

Eight body language techniques you'll find helpful are shown opposite.

On Day 8, we'll go into more detail on how to invent interesting gestures.

Work Out: Read Speech Through Once

After lunch, close your door and read through or give your talk off the cuff. From now on, till Day 10, jump at as many opportunities as possible to familiarize yourself with your talk.

> **Pro Pointer #65:** Frequent rehearsals *every few hours* will be far more potent than one two-hour rehearsal in giving your talk platform polish.

Also after lunch, think about this . . .

Be a Pumpkin-Changer

At a seminar for business people, a speaker told his listeners they could change pumpkins (their careers) into coaches by expressing desirable qualities. He pointed out, for instance, that if his listeners had an angry, dissatisfied customer, and treated him with sympathy, understanding, and liking, and corrected any mistakes the customer complained about, the customer would change. He'd become a desirable customer. He went on to point out that similar results could be obtained in expressing the right qualities in a boss-employee relationship as well.

1. In order to talk and gesture effectively, you must stand straight and strong. Stand on both feet, weight evenly distributed. Don't "dance"—that is, shift from foot to foot, go up and down on your toes and back on your heels, or list to one side with your weight on one foot. Lack of balance in standing and feet jitters make an audience extremely uncomfortable. You can conquer jitters by imagining a bag of concrete sandbagged across your feet or your feet nailed to the floor—not allowing you to move—unless you need to move to a blackboard, pick up a prop, etc.

2. When not using body language, keep hands at your side. It's the best place to start a gesture. If reading a talk, you can keep them *lightly* on the lectern, but don't rest your weight on them.

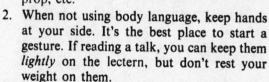

3, 4, 5. Ninety-five percent of your gestures are with your hands. Don't merely gesture with your right hand. Bring your left hand into play. And every now and then put both hands in motion, at once. Try for a *variety* of gestures.

6. You make your talk more visually compelling if every so often you hold up a prop— preferably a large one.

7. Remember, you also gesture with your head, your torso, your whole body. A lift of the eyebrows or a shrug of the shoulders can be a significant gesture. Don't stand at the lectern like an automaton who merely uses his hands.

8. Smiling and *glowing* as you talk is a form of body language. It telegraphs your enthusiasm to your audience. Whenever appropriate, smile. A well-known speaker used to say, "Audiences like happy, smiling speakers. Scowl and the audience will scowl with you."

The seminar speaker passed out miniature pumpkins to his listeners and advised them to keep them on their desks and look at them. "Remember," he said, "be a pumpkin-changer. Express qualities that turn your pumpkin into a coach. And enjoy a royal-coach career ride."

This anecdote has meaning for a speaker. When you step up to talk, expressing the right qualities will help change your audience's attitude from disinterest to warm interest.

So right now, start thinking about, as well as expressing, the qualities you want to bring out in your talk: attentiveness, alertness, sharing, appreciation of your message, friendliness, vigor, kindness, professionalism, etc. There are also many others.

Whipping Up Several Questions

Also before you go back to work after lunch, whip up several questions you can use to kick off the question-and-answer period.

If a silence falls when you ask for questions, throwing out a question or two of your own will give your listeners time to think of a query and help loosen their tongues. Often, good questions to ask concern points you didn't cover in your talk but which would interest the audience.

For example, Jerry might say:

While someone's thinking of a question, here's one I'll throw out to get things started. How much can a contractor expect to make with a well digging and pump program?

Or,

Here's a question that may have occurred to you. What kind of *growth* pattern do I see in the next five years of my business?

> Pro Pointer #66: The more *provocative* the questions you prepare, the more they'll interest your audience.

Delivering Your Introduction/Background Sheet/Publicity Release

After your office closes for Day 7 (and if you haven't already delivered them) get your introduction and background sheet, for the program chairman, and publicity release with picture, for the media, and drop them off on your way home. You'll find receptionists and guards at newspaper, TV, and radio stations most helpful. Just say, "Here's a release," and they'll grab your envelope and get it to the right people.

As you drive home, work on parts of your talk. Say the memorized head and feet or rehearse a nutshell point with its accompanying illustrative matter. It's more effective if you actually talk *aloud* in your car. But if you take a bus or train, you can rehearse mentally. However, I've also rehearsed aloud by simply telling a seatmate I'm rehearsing. Just recently, a well-known music critic said he rode into New York on a train with a woman who was softly rehearsing her part in the chorus of an opera.

At home, after dinner, spend an hour rehearsing before a mirror, using gestures and substituting visual aids.

Playing Before Your Home Audience

It takes guts to perform in front of your spouse before you finish polishing your talk. But the end results are worth the strain.

You'll find it's helpful to use the Critique Sheet in chapter 8. Show the Critique Sheet to your spouse. Brief him or her on how to fill it out according to the information in chapter 8. Then plunge in and give your talk, using body English and real or make-shift visual aids.

After you finish and receive a filled-in critique sheet, you'll begin to feel a warm glow—that while your talk needs to be smoother, it has some mighty good parts.

In Control: Programming for Your Second Wind

When you finish your performance before your home audience, *reward* yourself. It took *energy* to rehearse today. Put some energy back in by enjoying your favorite snack. Remember the ground rules, though. Once you finish going over your spouse's critique sheet, don't think about your talk the rest of the evening.

On Day 7, I find it really helps to think about the *big reward* you'll receive for delivering a first-rate talk. If you planned to give yourself a new tennis racket and perhaps have already purchased it, get it out. Swing it a few times. Haven't bought it yet but have a picture of it? Get that out. Study—and mentally swing—the pictured racket. Then relax the rest of the evening with an absorbing TV show or book.

Flashback

1. Whether rehearsing a talk you'll give off the cuff or one you'll read from cards, always say the head and feet from memory—*directly to your audience.*
2. In reading from cards, drop your eyes to the card (try not to bend your head), grab a line, raise your eyes to the audience, and repeat the line from recall. Use eye-contact to a variety of people in the audience 80% of the time.
3. In rehearsing an off-the-cuff talk, always give your illustrative material in the same order, but use fresh words each time you rehearse.
4. For either an off-the-cuff or "read" talk, speak *conversationally.*
5. Prepare several provocative questions you can ask if there's a lag at the start of the question-and-answer session.

DAY 8

How to Fast-Play
a Decisive Pre-match

Daily Step-Takers
- Work out alone
- Rehearsing before business friends
- Collecting comments
- Preparing a Q&A notebook

Things You'll Need
- Photocopied Critique Sheet
- Looseleaf notebook with subject tabs

A top golf teacher and analyst recently predicted a pro golfer would cop a major title and reach superstardom *if* he could learn not to tighten up under pressure. "He needs more exposure," said the teacher. "Exposure creates composure."

Indeed, exposure creates composure. That's why salesmen role-play before presentations, why board chairmen rehearse before annual meetings, and why, on Day 8, we rehearse, rehearse, rehearse.

Three Concentrated Read-Throughs

When you duck into your office, and while you quick-breakfast, get your visual aids—or make-shift ones—in place for a rehearsal. Arrange a few objects around your office as an "audience."

Now look over your spouse's critique sheet. If any of the suggestions seem valid, make changes in your talk. Then, as you sip your coffee, have three concentrated rehearsals. Remember to take five-minute breaks *in which you do something else.*

> **Pro Pointer #67:** In all, before Day 10,
> you should rehearse your "read" talk
> from 8 to 12 times; your off-the-cuff
> talk from 12 to 20 times.

Tips for Using Visual Aids Smoothly

As mentioned before, if you take a big-ticket-priced executive seminar or a series of talk lessons, you get, among other things, hints and aids that help you in making a fabulous pro talk.

Here are a few tips for using visual aids that will professionalize your speech:

1. *Use large visual aids that are easy to see and to understand.*
2. *Show all slides in one group.* It distracts the audience if you keep flicking a light on and off to show slides at various times.
3. *Employ the fill-in device.* Leave an important figure or fact blank on a chart. Then when you give that information, write it in at the same time. The result? A bit of effective show biz!
4. *Put pizzaz in your pointing.* Don't turn away from your audience to face a blackboard or chart in order to point to something on it. Rehearse till you can point deftly to something while *looking at and talking to the audience.*
5. *Simultaneous sight and sound.* Make sure, too, to point *at the same time* you say that fact or figure.
6. *Writing on a blackboard.* In rehearsals, practice till you

can write in a position *three-quarters facing your audience.* Try not to turn your back on your audience even to erase.

7. *Built-in prompter.* When you must use hard-to-remember figures, facts, or other information, write them lightly in the corner of your flip (or other) chart. You can even write in a nutshell point. You'll have a built-in prompter.

8. *Keep visual aids covered till you use them.* If you leave them uncovered, your audience will start looking at them and not heed what you're saying.

Eight Guides for Using/Inventing Skilled Body Talk

On Day 7 you learned basic techniques for employing body language. Often, in order to shine as a speaker, you must prepare part of your body talk in advance. Here are a few guides for doing so:

1. **Plan to employ large, forceful, action gestures.** Tailor your gestures to the size of your audience—the larger the group, the bigger your gestures. Make them forceful and action-filled. Put heft behind them. Don't gesture, for example, with just a hand flopping around from a wrist. If you move your hand, move your arm and put plenty of force behind that movement.

> **Pro Pointer #68:** *Forceful* body language makes you appear vigorous and vital.

2. **Vary your body language.** Want to drive your audience up the wall? Then employ only one or two favorite gestures— such as jabs with your right hand (or left, if you're a southpaw). If you use only one or two gestures over and over, it's monotonous, monotonous, monotonous.

Think, in advance, of varied body language you can use that fits your talk. For example: Do you want to describe how you often get your best business ideas as you drive down the freeway? Get those hands up there on an imaginary wheel, steer, and turn as you talk. Are you describing a problem with someone's archery shooting technique? Get your hands and arms up. Make an imaginary shot. *Show* your audience the problem.

Think of yourself as choreographing your body language. Aim to keep *varied* body language going throughout your talk.

> **Pro Pointer #69: Publius Syrus said,
> "No pleasure endures unseasoned
> by variety."**

3. Putting your eyeglasses to work. If you can get by reading your talk without glasses, do so. Glasses put a barrier between you and your audience. However, if you must use glasses, put them to work for you. Use them to point with, take them off and hold them in your hand when you wish to depart from your text for an off-the-cuff remark, even slip them on top of your head for a "different" visual effect.

> **Pro Pointer #70: Just as your speech
> sparkles with a mix of verbal illustrations,
> you must strive to give your listeners many
> *different* visual effects throughout your talk.**

4. Utilize signposting. Here's body talk no speaker can be without. Probably the most popular way to signpost is to raise one finger when you say, "My first point" . . . "My first reason . . ." "The first effect . . ." And when you raise that finger, hold up your whole arm in a bold gesture. Then, raise two fingers when you say, "My second point . . ." and so on.

> **Pro Pointer #71: Signposting is an
> easy, fun way to change from amateur
> to pro speaker.**

5. Apply informal gestures. Informal body language is good taste for contemporary audiences. Informal body action says to your listeners, "You're my friends. I like you. I have nothing to hide from you."

Recently, a business speaker rubbed his nose and later scratched his head, at the same time nodding with great interest as he listened to questions from the audience. Another business speaker, being honored for her contribution to her industry, waved to her friends in the audience.

6. Poker face? Liven up your expression. Business people need to work on varying their facial language. Quirk an eyebrow over a question. Give a quick grin if the subject matter merits it. Let your face soften or toughen, depending on the point you make.

A critic once summed up an actress' acting ability with, "She ran the gamut from A to B."

> **Pro Pointer #72: Let your expression run *more* than an A-to-B gamut.**

7. Talk with your whole body. A famed acting coach once told her students, "Acting's more than saying lines. It's a matter not so much of acting but of *reacting*. Work on reacting."

There are times in your talk when you can effectively talk with your whole body by reacting. *Example:* You can square your shoulders when you talk about being encouraged by a committee's accomplishments. To show how a piece of news "rocked you," you can rock back like a fighter who received a blow.

8. Let what you say help you invent the right body language. Don't use only the gestures others use. Create fresh, pertinent ones. How do you do so? Various ways. Start giving your talk with super-enthusiasm. Notice the spontaneous gestures you make. Keep the ones that seem fresh and vivid. Think about what you'll emphasize and what gesture you might come up with.

Example: What if Jerry, the contractor, wants to point out to his listeners that they can attract customers with either radio or newspaper advertising? He makes a *swiveling* gesture with his hand, indicating either media is okay. *Another example:* A woman exec, talking about how she wasn't warmly accepted in the male executive suite, hunched her shoulders, pulled up her jacket collar around her ears, and said, "I began to feel the atmosphere was *chilling*."

Inviting Business Friends to Play Audience

Before a company puts a product on the market, it studies what type of product the market needs or wants; it designs that type of product; tests it on various types of users; runs test advertising in test markets; and, when all the bugs are worked out, finally introduces it with national advertising to a national market. Today, a knowledgeable company gives itself its best chance—its best shot—to make it big with that product.

You, too, must test your product on an audience. So, later this morning plan to invite three or four of your business friends to hear your talk after lunch or over a sandwich in the conference room. If possible, invite the type of people who'll hear your talk. That is, if you'll speak to women consumers, invite women. An accounting audience? Ask your company accountants. However, if you can't duplicate the type of audience you'll speak to—don't worry. You can brief them so they'll step into the shoes of your upcoming audience and then their comments will aid you.

Using a Critique Sheet

About now you'll say, "That's a pretty tough thing to tackle—to speak to my business friends before I put the final spit and polish on my talk."

However, by using the Critique Sheet shown here, you won't find it difficult to speak before your friends at this stage. In fact it's easy, because you'll get their reactions via a helpful and *lucky* critique sheet. What makes this 13-question sheet lucky for all to use is its "impersonal" slant. Whoever fills it out discovers the questions refer to "the speaker," so a critic doesn't feel he's personally criticizing you. Nor will you feel personally criticized.

Briefing Your Business Friends

At lunchtime in the conference room with your visual aids, a lectern or lectern stand-in, and your assembled business friends, get ready to make your talk.

> **Pro Pointer #73: Describe to your friends the kind of audience you'll ultimately face. Ask them to judge your talk as if they were typical members of that audience.**

Critique Sheet

1. Did the speaker stand with his weight evenly distributed on both feet? _____
2. Should he talk louder?_____
3. Did he use varied eye-contact to all in the room? _____
4. If he read a talk, estimate what percentage of the time he looked at the audience. _____
5. Did he talk in a conversational way? _____ Or was he merely reading from his cards?_____
6. Was the opener fascinating?_____
7. Did the speech close with impact? _____
8. Did you like the verbal illustrative matter—anecdotes, statistics, jokes, etc.? _____
9. Any of this you didn't like? Name _____
10. Were the visual aids large enough and understandable? _____ If not, how could the speaker improve his visual aids? _____
11. Did the speaker use body language? _____ Did he gesture singly with *each* hand, as well as with both in unison?_____
12. Is there anything you didn't understand in this presentation? _____ What was it? _____
13. Do you have any advice for the speaker? _____

Assure them, too, that they needn't hesitate to fill out the critique sheet you'll pass out after your talk. Explain that, because of its impersonal reference to "the speaker," their comments won't hurt your feelings and they needn't pull their punches. Tell them frankness instead of flattery can help you pinpoint a weakness and get rid of it.

> **Pro Pointer #74: Tape your talk.**

The Art of Turning On

When you give your talk to your office audience, really "turn on"—become enthusiastic. How do you know if you've turned on? You'll recall that when people are really enthusiastic about what they're saying their faces glow. Be so interested in what you're saying that your face will *glow*.

Your High-Intensity Pre-match

Turning on in this manner, go through your talk with as much high intensity and style as if you were giving the talk before your future audience. Go through "the works." Use body language, visual aids (or make-shifts), strong eye-contact.

As you talk, you'll begin to sense your audience is your partner. They're *with* you. You'll see their reactions, hear them laugh at your jokes, and see their quickening of interest over certain illustrations. While you realize you still need to polish your talk, you will probably feel marvelously heartened. You'll feel like racing ahead and putting on the finishing touches!

Fielding Q&A's

Ask for questions. Field any that your business friends toss at you. If they don't readily ask a question, practice throwing out a couple you've prepared to get things going. Tomorrow, I'll give you specific tips to help you handle your questions with professional aplomb.

Collecting Comments

Collect the critique sheets from your business friends. Also pay attention to any verbal comments they make. A purchasing agent I know, holding this type of audience prematch, found his listeners were still asking questions as the session broke up. He realized he had an unusually interesting talk on collecting modern photographs as a profitable hobby.

A textile manager, after her prematch, received praise for her speech. One audience member, as she was leaving the room, said, "You amaze me. I never thought you could speak so well. Honestly, you were sensational!" The textile manager felt assured she'd put together an outstanding presentation.

Both people, much encouraged, went on to add the final polish to their talk.

Assessing Your Strengths and Weaknesses

When the workday ends, relax over a Coke and take a few minutes before you leave to review your critique sheets and assess your strengths and weaknesses. Tomorrow, you can act on any criticism you feel is valid by making changes in your talk.

Preparing a Q&A Notebook

After your trial run today, you may feel you need certain factual information—such as figures, facts, quotes from authorities—at your fingertips to consult or read from in answering questions. So do as some wise talkers do. Make a Q&A notebook. Put this information under alphabetical headings. With tape and paper, you can make a pocket on a notebook sheet and put a brochure or chart in it.

On a television program recently, two spokesmen for a certain industry continuously consulted their Q&A notebooks to read convincing facts and figures they would not have been able to carry in their heads.

> **Pro Pointer #75: Referring to a Q&A notebook helps you appear credible, well organized, and able to defend your company's position.**

In Control: Score by Taking It Easy

Tonight you may wish to rehearse once or twice before a mirror. But remember, don't rehearse after 9:00 p.m. Take it easy, enjoy a snack, watch TV, take a short walk, or read a thriller— whatever relaxes you. But don't think about your talk. Tomorrow, on Day 9, you'll learn the little miracle workers that can effectively tighten up your talk for the *big day*.

Flashback

1. When you rehearse at various times today, use visual aids, body language, eye-contact.
2. How many times should you work out before Day 10? With a "read" speech from 8 to 12 times. Off the cuff, rehearse from 12 to 20 times.
3. When you play a prematch before your business friends, picture yourself as glowing with enthusiasm. This helps you turn on.
4. Pass out a photocopied Critique Sheet to each of your friends. Collect their comments after your talk.
5. In line with these comments, make any needed changes.
6. Prepare a Q&A notebook that lists information—facts, figures, quotes from authorities—you may need in fielding questions.

Little Miracle Workers Tighten Your Talk —And Your Inner Drive

Daily Step-Takers
- Revise talk
- Work out
- Q&A drill
- Assemble visual aids

Things You'll Need
- Talk cards
- Q&A notebook
- Visual aids
- Tape recorder

You may remember the legend about the church whose chimes would not peal till a gift of love was placed on the altar. A procession of rulers and wealthy men put jewels and gifts of great wealth there but the church bells remained silent.

Then one Christmas Eve, a beggar boy, virtually unnoticed by the important people bearing gifts, stole down the aisle of the church, went to the altar, took off his threadbare coat, and placed it there. Chimes rang out to mark the unselfish gift of the lad.

While you can't compare the poor little lad's placing his coat on the altar to your giving your talk, there is an analogy. On Day 9 by carrying through with the following steps for the benefit of your listeners, you will make your talk special for your audience . . . you will help make chimes ring for them.

Play Back Yesterday's Talk

As you eat your portable breakfast, listen to and time the recording of yesterday's talk before your business friends. Make a note of the time. As you listen, keep in mind any pertinent comments from the critique sheets you received. Note any point that didn't go over well. Was it clear enough? Did you lack illustrative material? For example: A distribution manager, reading his critique sheets, found that he did *not* get a totally favorable reaction. His listeners said they were bored with one of his points. Cannily, he edited out this part and beefed up another that the listeners liked. The result? He turned a near disaster into a triumph.

> **Pro Pointer #76: Make any necessary changes to strengthen your talk.**

Next, consider if you should make any changes in your delivery. Should some part be spoken faster? Some slower? Some softer? Some louder? Should you put more "color" into your voice? When you say "profits," for example, should you make the word sound more desirable?

> **Pro Pointer #77: Putting *variety* into your delivery can help turn a talk from sounding wobbly to *wow*.**

Notice if you slur any words or drop final consonants to the extent that you cannot be understood. If so, as you rehearse, spend a few minutes at the close of each workout saying the problem word or words 10 to 15 times, emphasizing the right pronunciation.

Make Any Necessary Changes

Mark your cards as shown on Day 7's symbol chart. And resolve to make any *delivery* corrections necessary to strengthen your talk.

Precision-Timing Your Talk

Now consider the time you clocked on your recorded talk. Timing is crucial. In fact, on Day 9, I like to point out to speakers how one business person, who founded a giant advertising agency, made *precision timing* work for him.

When the executive wanted to make a presentation or discuss something with a business person, he would call and ask for "9 minutes" or "14 minutes" or "23 minutes" to talk with him. Entering the office, the advertising executive would put his watch on the table in front of him, and look at it frequently as he talked. In *exactly* the number of minutes he asked for, he would skillfully deliver a well-planned presentation. His awareness of time, and mental organization, set the stage and made a tremendous impression on business people he called on.

Coming in on time (or a little under) will act as a small miracle worker in your talk's success. If you need to cut your talk, it's easy to do. Just follow this rule-of-thumb:

Rule-of-Thumb for Cutting a Talk

Generally, cut a whole point and its illustrations if you need to reduce a talk by more than five minutes. If you need to cut only three or four minutes, drop an illustration or two.

Should you need to chop out only two or three minutes (200-300 words), go through and cut paragraphs, sentences, and words that can be spared.

For instance, Jerry, the contractor, might spot a sentence like: "You'll find advertising in the Yellow Pages can bring you good dividends." He might trim this to: "You'll find Yellow Pages advertising works."

"Why all this talk about shortening my speech?" you ask, as you look up from munching your Danish and drinking coffee. "What if my talk does run 10 or 15 minutes over? After all, I'm not performing brain surgery. I won't kill anybody by running overtime." My answer to that is you kill your speaking reputation when you talk too long.

> **Pro Pointer #78: Don't risk blemishing your career by letting your time at the lectern get out of control.**

Occasionally, you may find you've come up with a five-minute talk and the program chairman arranged with you for a 15-minute one. If you need to pad, add illustrations. However, don't pad till you achieve a 15-minute talk. Compromise and make it a 10- or 12-minute speech.

> **Pro Pointer #79: Often, even better than an accurately timed talk is one that comes in *under* the time limit.**

The wit Irvin S. Cobb said, "No speech can be entirely bad if it's short enough." And even if you have a blockbuster talk, the advice of a famous speaker, "Be brief, be interesting, be seated," is still the best advice.

Working Out with Miracle-Style Delivery

Remember the Latin inscription Benjamin Franklin recommended for the dollar bill: *Annuit coeptus.* It translates: be favorable to bold enterprises. Franklin chose this motto because he knew that new enterprises, new businesses, new tactics, could make America's economy grow.

To make your talk grow and prosper, *boldly* put into effect the points mentioned above. And as you work out today and tomorrow, boldly continue the use of these little miracle workers—correct eye-contact, visual aids, body language, and conversational manner of talking.

Working Out with 80% Head-Up Delivery

From now on as you work out, if you read a talk try to look at your audience 80% of the time.

> **Pro Pointer #80: Eighty-percent eye-contact with the audience, when you read a talk, velvetizes and vitalizes your performance.**

Naturally, if you talk off the cuff maintain 100% eye-contact.

Clues for a Winning Q&A Session

There's a strong trend developing in talking: talks are growing shorter, Q&A periods longer, and questions *tougher!*

Since more and more people today think of preparing and delivering an outstanding talk as part of their job, they're anxious to handle Q&A's with a pro touch. In order to handle a Q&A well, a speaker must not let it get out of control.

Following are highly important tips for keeping a *firm* hand on your Q&A. Note especially the useful Quickie Recipe for Breaking with the Questioner.

> **Quickie Recipe for Breaking with the Questioner**
>
> 1. If someone wishes to ask a question, turn and face him. Acknowledge he has the floor by a nod and smile, or a remark pointing him out.
> 2. Listen with *complete* attention to the question . . . and how you will clarify or brief it when you repeat it. (Don't think about the answer.) Keep a poker face over a rude question. An especially apt or amusing question? Flatter your listener with a smile, nod of approval, and "That's a good question."
> 3. Before you answer, turn and face another part of the audience, and repeat the question.

Don't depart from this protocol. It can add tremendous polish to the Q&A session. Unless it's a small group, never turn back to the questioner and say, "Did I answer your question?" Assume you have. If you haven't, he'll talk to you after the meeting. Later today I'll give you tips for handling hostile questions.

Buying Thinking Time

Why do you turn and face a *different* part of the audience and repeat the question before answering it? There are several reasons. One is that this procedure lets you buy *thinking time*.

A well-known speaking coach says, "We think about 300 times faster than we talk." So in those few seconds of turning away to face another part of the audience, you are buying a nice hunk of time to think out your answers.

The Special Recipe for an Apt Answer on page 127 will help you speed-think *quality* answers to many questions you'll field.

Try Using the "How-Can-I-Help-You" Trick

Besides the special recipe just given for answering questions, another helpful thing to keep in mind is the how-can-I-help-you trick.

You know how pleased you are when you find a salesperson who's not so interested in selling you something as he is in helping you solve a problem. This help-you attitude brings you back to that salesperson— and you give him your future business.

If you can get rid of thinking that a questioner has asked a "dumb question," a "tough question," or a "he's-out-to-get-me-or-my-company question" and replace it with a how-can-I-help-you attitude, you can come off well in fielding questions.

To foster this attitude, follow these tips:

First, do your homework. Anticipate questions. One authority maintains you can anticipate 85% of the questions asked. So jot down questions you might encounter and figure out answers.

Second, have facts, figures, and quotes from authorities at your fingertips—often in the form of the Q&A notebook mentioned earlier. Be generous about giving a questioner a helpful fact or figure.

Special Recipe for an Apt Answer

Many times you can use this recipe to make an *on-target* answer—instead of muddling through a reply.

1. In answering a question, start out with a statement that gives your position or point of view. For example, Jerry, the contractor, might receive a question like this:

> While you may make a good income with a water well program, you probably work a seven-day week. Do you ever get any recreation?

Jerry would answer first by stating his position on the question. He answers:

> Yes, I get a lot of recreation.

2. Next, give your reason-why for your position or point of view. This can be a specific fact, figure, quote from an authority, or often a concrete example from your own experience. Jerry might say:

> For example, I have a farm with a tenant farmer and I get up there many weekends to lie around and hunt and fish. And last Christmas I took my family on a 10-day tour of the Holy Land.

Notice, to make his point, Jerry doesn't ramble on, mentioning every trip and every form of recreation he takes. Just one or two *concrete* examples will do it.

3. Finally, restate your position or point of view. Jerry might say:

> So along with a good income, I definitely enjoy recreation. I believe other water well contractors will find they can, too.

Third, plan to be *extra* helpful, whenever feasible, and volunteer to give the questioner added information, if he will get in touch with you later. Always follow through on providing this information.

Follow These Stop-and-Go's

When you drive your car, stop and go signals help you drive better. The stop-and-go's which follow will help you answer questions better:

• *Stop*. Don't get sidetracked in your answer. Determine the *main premise* of your reply. Stick to it. Don't ramble.

• *Go*. Try to keep your answers *brief*.

• *Stop*. Don't get in a quarrel with a questioner. Remain pleasant, courteous, unflappable. Remember, psychologically speaking, when someone picks a quarrel with you he usually wants to gain the spotlight for himself. When you can, say something complimentary to him—perhaps about his question.

• *Go*. If you know the questioner's name, use it a couple of times when answering. Don't know his name? If appropriate, ask. Then use it. Throw in a warm phrase or two. "As Miss Carpenter so well put it . . ." or "I think our friend John Askew has a real point here . . ."

• *Stop*. Don't harshly correct a questioner. Often, a questioner may have the wrong facts. Start your answer to him with a sympathetic kick-off like, "I can well understand Bob Roundtree's concern. But Bob and some of you may not be aware of these factors." Then set forth correct facts. Never adopt the tone of "setting nuts straight." Your attitude should always indicate a modest aim to "let the truth appear."

• *Go*. If you can give a witty but kindly answer, do so. Don't, however, give a flippant reply or put-down. This usually harms your image.

• *Stop*. Don't be afraid to say "I don't know" when you're stumped. It's preferable to trying to bull your way through an answer. But whenever possible, say you'll get the answer for the questioner. Remember, it's that how-can-I-help-you attitude that will help make you the speaker a group will want to have again.

• *Go*. Sometimes a questioner will challenge you on something you've said—and he's right. Admit it. Say, "You're absolutely right." If it's something that doesn't particularly matter to the assembled group, ask him to talk with you after the meeting.

Handling Hostile Questioners

Some listeners attend talks armed with facts and figures—and they ask angry, accusatory questions. Such questioners lack courtesy. They ask what one business writer calls "the getcha" questions— carefully framed questions posed with an air of "Now I'll get you!"

Adroit speakers, however, can often defuse antagonistic questions, and at the same time help achieve a better relationship with their listeners. How do they do this? The Tips for Answering Hostile Questioners will give you useful hints.

Tips for Handling
Hostile Questioners

- Follow the protocol given earlier for turning from the questioner to another part of the audience before answering the question.
- Be *careful* not to get a debate going between yourself and the questioner. Often, audiences can't hear a speaker-questioner debate—and this back and forth exchange bores listeners.
- Slipping into a debate takes the power out of your hands—and puts it in the questioner's hands. Outwit the power grabber.
- Novelist John Steinbeck once said, "An answer is invariably the parent of a great family of new questions." By turning away, not giving an answer directly to the questioner, you squelch a great family of new questions. It's usually not the first, but the second, third, or fourth question that embarrasses a speaker, causes him to squirm, grope, and come off badly in his Q&A.
- Accepting a variety of questions from *various* people often prevents a hostile situation from arising.
- Refuse to take offense at a personal or violent attack. Rephrase it as a question, depersonalizing it. Remain impersonal in your answer. Concentrate on giving a factual answer.
- The more hostile the questioner, the more specific the facts and figures you must provide to satisfy him.

Foolproof Assembling of Your Visual Aids

After your office shuts down for the day and you relax with a Coke or a candy bar, assemble your visual aids. Here are points to consider in assembling and checking them out:

✓ Check their condition. Do any look smudged? Clean gummy spots with a gum eraser. Tape everything that's loose.

✓ If you'll leave from home tomorrow to make your talk, get your visual aids into your car tonight and see that no one in the family disturbs them.

✓ If you leave them in the office, put your visual aids under lock and key. You don't want a colleague walking off with them when he borrows the office portfolio.

✓ Using slides? See that they're intact and in order. Bringing your projector? Get it ready now. *Try it out.* Also pack an extra projector bulb.

Just as you get a tune-up for your car, this is tune-up time for your visual aids. See that they're ready *now* to go with you tomorrow.

Also, if you haven't already done so, number your talk cards in the upper right-hand corner. Then in case you drop them, you can quickly put them in order again. Leave your cards with a note for your secretary to type your talk in manuscript style, double-spaced, on 8½" × 11" white bond. Specify the number of copies you'll need to hand out to any external media editors, company house organ editor, club secretary, and anyone else who might need a copy.

Like Your Inner Golf Game

As you may know if you play golf, you play two games. You play the outer game with techniques for drives, putting, etc. And you play the inner game of keeping your nerves under control and yourself psyched up to play your best.

You've readied your talk's outer game. From now on your biggest concern will be your inner game—how *not* to get distracted, how to stay loose, how to keep pretalk nerves and fear from taking over. In fighting talk fear, remember even the best and most experienced talkers suffer from talk jitters. Tomorrow we'll show you how to jitter-proof yourself.

Jerry Bascomb
President
Jerry Bascomb, Inc.
P.O. Box 399
Pacetown, N.C. (Zip)
(Phone number)
(Date)

*Release after (give time and
date of talk)*

HOW TO ATTRACT PROFITABLE NEW
WELL AND PUMP CUSTOMERS

(Following is the text of remarks by Jerry Bascomb,
president, Jerry Bascomb, Inc., before a seminar of the
National Association of Contractors in Las Vegas, on day,
month, year of talk.)
    Begin text . . .

But I've found there are some things you can do now to make yourself far more comfortable before a talk. For example . . .

Allowed: A Four-Ingredient Gratitude Cocktail

Though alcohol is out today and on Day 10 if you want to give a blockbuster talk, let me urge you to try this four-ingredient gratitude cocktail. Mix and sip it before you leave for home tonight.

- Feel gratitude for the help of others—your family, your office colleagues—who've helped you with your talk's preparation.
- Feel gratitude that you've had the time to plan and rehearse your talk.
- Feel gratitude that you're now *well prepared.*
- Feel gratitude that your talk will get across points to others that will *help* or entertain them.

Gratitude takes your thought off yourself, gives you a good inner feeling, and is a potent relaxer.

In Control: Setting Your Inner Thermostat for Success

When dinner's finished, hold a Q&A drill. Ask your spouse to throw out a few of the questions you prepared in your homework earlier. Answer them with the miracle-power techniques.

After 9:00 p.m., set your inner thermostat for big success in two ways:

- On a sheet of paper write, "I won't think about my talk till tomorrow." Crumple it into a ball and throw it in the wastebasket. If you find your thought drifting back to your talk, mentally retoss the talk "ball" into the basket.
- Lace one cup of hot milk with one teaspoon of honey. Sip slowly. Many speakers find this nightcap helps them sleep better.

Even if you don't sleep too much tonight, don't be concerned. Simply keep your thought off any problems and on pleasant things. You'll be fresh for tomorrow's target-hitter tips that will let you splendidly put across your talk.

Flashback

1. Make any changes needed in your talk.
2. In your Q&A session, observe this protocol: Turn and face the questioner. Listen with *complete* attention to his question (don't think about the answer). Next, turn to another part of the audience, repeat the question (often rephrasing it for clarity or brevity), and answer it.
3. While you're restating the question, you're buying time to quickly think out a possible answer.
4. In answering questions, here's a helpful recipe: (a) state your position or stand, (b) cite a fact, figure, quote from an authority, or something from your own experience to substantiate your stand, and (c) end by restating your position or point of view.
5. Remain courteous, friendly, unflappable.

How to Employ
Target-Hitter Tips
to Score a Winning Speech

Daily Step-Takers
- Limit: three rehearsals
- Cultivate inner harmony
- Use "pro" delivery
- Hand out take-away kits

Things You'll Need
- Visual aids
- Take-away kits

As you sit at your desk with your carry-in breakfast on Day 10, think for a minute about the proverb that says: "He who works with his hands is a laborer. He who works with his hands and his head is a craftsman. He who works with his hands, his head, and his heart is an artist."

Now the hours are winding down to a precious few before

your talk. And during these next few hours you'll see how to bring out the artistry in delivering an effective talk.

Caution: Don't Rehearse More Than Three Times

An insurance saleswoman learned the hard way not to over-rehearse. On Day 9 she gave a tremendous talk before her office peers. She awoke on Day 10 and decided to make a good thing better by rehearsing *all* during the day—up to the time of her talk. What happened? She became fagged out. The result? She gave a poor talk without sparkle.

On Day 10, to be at your most sparkling best, don't rehearse more than three times.

> **Pro Pointer #81: The third rehearsal, if possible, should be within two hours of your talk.**

How to Shake "Ingratituditis"

On Day 10, just as you're about to win the rewards for your faithful work on your talk, you may discover that ingratituditis will try to creep in. You may find yourself feeling resentful because you had to prepare visual aids, work out with body language, take time away from other pressing matters. Don't let ingratituditis sink your talk.

> **Pro Pointer #82: Rout ingratituditis by enjoying another gratitude cocktail now.**

Three Guidelines to Turning Off at Work

An executive once said that when he's occupied with thinking about something he occasionally likes to become anonymous, melt into the crowd, not attract attention. When he's in Paris, he says, he can do this by wearing a workingman's cap. Nobody pays any attention to him. In fact, taxis won't even stop for him.

So you'll be fresh for your talk, you *don't* want to attract attention today. Here are three guidelines for not getting involved at work:

1. Don't feed conversations. The best way to avoid this is usually to just nod and smile pleasantly. Don't make in-depth comments or ask questions.
2. Don't visit a branch or call on a customer, if you can help it.
3. Don't *initiate* anything today—postpone starting a demanding new task or holding six-month performance reviews. Simply do routine work.

> **Pro Pointer #83: People sabotage their talks—and often quite a bit of their future reputation—by getting overly involved in their work on the day of their talk.**

Two Aids for Inner Harmony

It's axiomatic—you never get a harmonious result from an inharmonious cause. So, as you sip your second cup of coffee before your office opens, think about two aids for harmonizing your thinking and shutting out fear before your talk. Whenever you start to feel tense:

1. Remind yourself you're well prepared. Remind yourself that in the past, being well prepared in various activities has led you to success. The good preparation you've done will have the same results for you today.
2. Give yourself a pep talk along these lines:

> To stop talk jitters I will be completely absorbed in my *subject* when I give my talk today.
> By keeping my thought completely on the ideas I present, it can't wander to myself. So, I *can't* be self-conscious.

> **Pro Pointer #84: This second tip—keeping thought entirely *focused* on your speech subject when you talk—is one of the most potent remedies known for stopping speech jitters.**

It will also serve to keep your audience's attention focused on what you're *saying,* instead of on you personally.

Early Ducking-Out Advice

• Make your game plan when you need to leave your office to give yourself *plenty* of time to get to your location. Keep to it.

• Decide now what you'll do in emergencies. Will you take a telephone call from a client as you're leaving the office? Will you go to a hastily called meeting thirty minutes before you leave?

A doctor who writes about turning off tension often makes this point: "The telephone rings. But you don't have to answer it." This is not only true of dealing with tension, but literally. My own thought is that when I'm booked to leave for a talk, I don't take phone calls or go to meetings thirty minutes before I leave. It isn't worth the effort I've put into the talk to arrive late or upset over something that's happened in a meeting.

> Pro Pointer #85: Accepting a last-minute telephone call or attending a hastily called meeting doesn't help you up the ladder of success the way a well-delivered talk does.

Pro-Style Setting Up

As you enter the premises of your talk, confer first with the program chairman. Ask if he has any special directive he'd like to give you. Check the lectern. Sometimes someone forgets to put it in place. Try the mike. Put your visual aids in the safe place you determined earlier.

Being Well Organized Helps Your Credibility

Organize your visual aids in the *order* you'll use them. Your charts should be in order and *covered* till you use them. Anything you can put on a blackboard ahead of time should be taken care of—and the blackboard covered till you need it.

> Pro Pointer #86: Good organization of your visual aids and props builds your credibility with your listeners.

A Seminar Leader's Advice

A successful seminar leader points out that a speaker's role begins when he arrives to give a talk. To psych yourself up to give an A+ talk, he advises thinking of yourself as the *host* of the meeting.

As *host* you will smile, appreciate the guests, be affable, and extremely interested in all who attend. If there's a cocktail hour, as a busy host you'll merely have a soft drink or tomato juice. You won't try, either, to be the life of the party and hold forth with a lot of stories. You'll save your stories for later when you talk.

If it's a long cocktail session, most speakers find it helps to dissipate tension if they move about physically. Perhaps you can help locate someone in the crowd who's wanted on the phone. Or perhaps you can recheck your visual aids.

> Pro Pointer #87: From time to time, silently say the memorized head and feet of your speech.

Mike Quickies

While you are seated and waiting to speak, review these points for using a mike:

1. If the mike's a standing one, see that it's the right height for you.
2. Keep an even distance from the mike—usually about 8 to 12 inches from a standing mike.
3. Don't turn away from the mike or your voice will fade out. Use eye-contact, but move your eyes rather than making extreme head movements.
4. If you get any hissing noises—sometimes because of using words with "s" in them, sometimes because of dentures—turn your head so you don't talk straight into the mike but *across* its face.
5. Don't talk as loudly as you would without a mike. Talk conversationally, as mentioned earlier. The mike is an intimate medium.

Four Steps to Personal Warmth

As you are seated before giving your talk, follow these steps to personal warmth:

1. Look out from time to time at various members of your audience with a pleasant smile. Don't keep your head buried in your plate or your notes.
2. Continue to think of yourself as the *host* of the meeting. Enter into things. Laugh at the other speakers' jokes. Listen with interest to even the most tedious reports. Talk to the persons on either side of you. The more interested and *outward-focused* your thought, the less nervous you'll become and the better the talk you'll deliver.
3. From time to time, mentally review the memorized head and feet and other parts of your talk.
4. Every so often look at your audience and think, "I *love* my audience."

> **Pro Pointer #88: With these prespeech preliminaries you set yourself up to deliver a blockbuster talk.**

12 Give-Aways for Glow-Power

You've worked for nine days with your hands and head to put together this talk. Now these *give-aways* will help you put the artistry—the *heart*—into it:

1. Give a smile and thanks to your introducer when you stand up.
2. Give your audience reassurance that you won't talk too long by putting down a timer or a clock.
3. Give a slow, approving look around the room. Don't be in a hurry to start talking.

A tour director, taking groups to view Eurpoean sights and scenery, found if he began speaking when the group first saw a new sight, they heard nothing he said. They were too busy looking. Later, as an in-demand business speaker, he discovered the same thing held true—his audience needed a minute or two to look him over.

4. Give a verbal pat on the back to your introducer—perhaps for his introduction. Sometimes a story is in order. At a recent marketing seminar, a speaker thanked his introducer and then said to the audience:

> Harry's a heck of a salesman. Terrific marketeer. He invited me to go shark fishing on his boat. We did and he fell off. But everything was okay. Sharks didn't touch him. Professional courtesy.

5. Give honor to the audience by considering their comfort and paying them a compliment or two, as indicated in the ice-breakers section of Treasure Chest # 1 on page 146.

6. Give your audience a feeling you're relaxed—so they can relax. How? By moving around a bit, adjusting your visual aids, or using body language as you talk informally in the preliminaries.

> **Pro Pointer #89: Famed composer Richard Rodgers advised actress Cloris Leachman to banish paralyzing jitters by taking a *deep breath* before singing or talking.**

7. Give out vibes of warmth.   Think of yourself as *mentally putting your arms around* your audience and saying to them, "I have some helpful things to share with you today."

8. Give your listeners a polished performance by delivering your talk as you rehearsed it—with energy and vitality. If something arises (perhaps an earlier speaker talked too long) and you need to cut your talk, remember the rules for cutting which you learned on Day 9.

9. Give your audience the pro treatment if you make a speaking boo-boo—perhaps mispronounce a word or omit some material—and realize it a sentence later. Don't stop. Go right on. Many times with an omission, the listeners never know the difference. If you try to backtrack, you often make another mistake.

10. Give your audience a break.   Don't worry them with a display of nervousness. Overcome nerves by keeping your thought focused on what you're saying. If you start to wonder, "How am I doing?" or "Do my listeners like my talk so far?" grab your thought and force it back to the subject of your talk.

> **Pro Pointer #90: Keeping your mind on your subject will iron out any shakiness you may feel.**

11. **Give out an air of enthusiasm.**

> **Pro Pointer #91: If two speakers are evenly prepared, the one who can get up and *glow with enthusiasm* over his subject and the opportunity to talk to an audience will be rated the superior talker—and he'll walk off with career rewards, too.**

12. **Give your listeners a *punchy* ending.** Take a step forward as you say your ending. If you're behind a lectern, lean forward and deliver your ending with vigor. Keep your voice *up.* When you talk, *GIVE!*

Conducting a High-Impact Q&A

Be just as professional about your question-and-answer period as your talk. If necessary, throw out a prime-the-pump question or two you've prepared.

> **Pro Pointer #92: Don't let the Q&A run longer than you and the chairman have agreed upon—often about eight or nine minutes.**

You'll notice the Q&A often starts with a few questions, builds up to a peak with several people wishing to ask questions at once, then the questions dwindle. If you've not received a Q&A time limit, usually cut the session off shortly after the peak question period.

Handing Out a Take-Away Kit

Close your Q&A period by saying, "The program chairman is signaling our time is up . . ." And then mention: "Don't forget, I have some hand-out material that may interest you." (Hold up a sample.) "It's here on the table. Help yourself."

In a talk before a club or organization, it's also courteous to say, "If a fourth-estater, house organ editor, or this organization's secretary would like a written copy of my speech, here it is." (Casually wave a couple of copies.)

Reaping Your Reward

You've built several success "highs" into your talk—your punchy closing, your Q&A, volunteering hand-out material, offering a written copy of your talk to the press, so if possible try to end on one more *high*. If you have a *brief,* amusing story, tell it. Smile, turn away, and shake hands with the program chairman.

> **Pro Pointer #93: You'll reap a big reward of applause . . . and add a nice notch in your climb up the ladder.**

Should You Turn Pro?

Nothing breeds success like manufacturing and delivering a really successful speech. One *outstanding* talk and the word gets around—back to your peers, your boss, members of your industry. You receive other *coveted* speaking invitations. Opportunities to lead workshops and seminars. Then you may find yourself faced with another problem and wondering: Should I turn pro? Or at least semi-pro?

Humorist Robert Benchley turned his talk about a company's profits into a well-paying lecture. A scientist who liked to talk in friends' living rooms on UFOs now does it for a living. A businesswoman-gardener makes enough from her talks to spend a few weeks a year traveling around the world studying famous gardens. Fees for hired tongues range from $100 to $5000 per appearance, plus expenses.

If your talks to business groups go well, why not expand? Try the paid lecture circuit. You can register with a local speakers' bureau. . . and perhaps accept 15 or 20 talk invitations a year to start with. A manufacturer's representative I know is doing just this. He finds many business groups want him. Eventually he plans to turn full-time pro. You might like to follow a similar course.

But whether you decide to become a pro supermouth or continue as an amateur supertalker, I'd like to remind you of Cicero's words: "The precept, 'Know yourself,' was not solely intended to obviate the pride of mankind; but likewise that we might understand our own worth." If you've put into practice the tips in this book, I believe you'll now know yourself as a speaker, and *like what you know!*

TREASURE CHEST 1

Actual Titles, Ice-Breakers, Bridges, Openers and Closers for Miracle Speech Power

Need an instant speech subject or title? Care to keep a few ice-breakers and speech bridges in your hip pocket? And what about an opener and/or closer for your talk? The following pages are your answer pages.

Titles That Spark Ideas

Scanning the titles which follow can provide you with an idea for a speech subject.

Example: David, the architect mentioned in chapter 1, looking over the list of titles which follow, sees title 4, "Aluminum: A Growth Industry." This triggers a speech idea: to talk about a growth field—historical restoration—to a meeting of architects.

Reading over this section will also provide inspiration for titling your talk.

Example: You decide to give a talk on getting innovative ideas in business. You browse through the titles and spot #13,

"Going to the Money Well." You pull the old switcheroo and title your talk, "Going to the Idea Well."

You'll find that the capitalized titles which follow are titles of *actual* talks, workshops, and seminars given to business and community groups. Below these capitalized titles I have placed two brainstorming titles which show the ideas the capitalized title suggested to me. I'm sure these title variations will spark a twist you can develop for your title. This list will also remind you of touches that make titles shine—including the use of short, snappy titles, provocative questions, alliteration, and rhyming titles such as title #20, "Out of the Hole with Coal."

1. A CREATIVE DIRECTOR LOOKS AT PRODUCTION COSTS
   A Contractor Looks at Tomorrow's Building Costs
   Headhunter Costs: The Pros and Cons
2. ALCOA'S PROGRAM FOR PROGRESS
   A Program for Executive Progress
   Your Company's Learning/Earning Program
3. ALICE IN ADVERTISING LAND
   Alice in Accounting Land
   Welcome to the New Land of Accounting
4. ALUMINUM: A GROWTH INDUSTRY
   Veterinary Services: A Growth Field
   Backgammon: Fast-Growing Hobby
5. ATTITUDE AND SUCCESS— INSEPARABLE PARTNERS
   Innovation and Success—Inseparable Partners
   Innovation Spells Success
6. BUSIER WHEN YOU RETIRE
   Busier When You Begin (Advice to graduates starting in business)
   Don't Retire—Re-tread!
7. CATERPILLAR IS PEOPLE
   Brown & Co. Is People
   People *Make* Our Business
8. EFFECTIVE NEGOTIATING
   Effective Jogging
   "Everybody Wins" Negotiating

9. EFFECTIVELY MANAGING YOUR TIME
   Effectively Managing Your Department
   S-T-R-E-T-C-H Your Time
10. EXPLORING THE WORLD AROUND US
    Exploring the World of Fast-Food Franchises
    How to Mine Business-Advice Books
11. FINANCING, DEVELOPING, PRESERVING
    YOUR BUSINESS
    Financing, Developing, Preserving Your Home
    Developing a Durable Business
12. FLYING SAUCERS ARE REAL
    Dissatisfied Customers Are Real
    The Real Cash-Flow Problem
13. GOING TO THE MONEY WELL
    Going to the Knowledge Well
    Priming Your Profits
14. HIDDEN DISSUADERS
    Hidden Stock Market Dissuaders
    Your Job's Five Hidden Advantages
15. HOW TO MINIMIZE RISKS AND MAXIMIZE
    SUCCESS WHEN INTRODUCING A NEW
    PRODUCT
    Maximizing Your Business Success
    Maximizing Your Success When Opening a New Outlet
16. HOW TO USE SPORTS IN SALES PROMOTION
    How to Use Role-Playing in Presentations
    How a Recording Star Can Highlight an Opening
17. LOOKING AT YOUR FUTURE
    Looking at a Young Dentist's Future
    Looking at a Pet Dealer's Profits
18. THE MONEYMAKERS
    Convenience Store Moneymakers
    Gemology: The Moneymaking Hobby
19. ONE PERSON CAN MAKE A DIFFERENCE—
    YOU
    You Can Make a Difference in Fund Raising
    The Metal Tennis Racket—and You!
20. OUT OF THE HOLE WITH COAL
    Out of the Hole with a Tax Dole
    Tips for Getting Your Club Out of the Hole

21. PROFOUND DESIGN CHANGES AHEAD
Profound Metric Changes Ahead
Social Security Changes Ahead for You
22. RETAIL RELIGION
Real Estate Religion
Revolution in Retailing
23. STRATEGY OF BUYING DURING UNUSUAL TIMES
Strategy of Selling During Unusual Times
Today's Winning Selling Strategy
24. THE SCHOOLMASTER AND HIS PUBLICS
The Banker and His Public Relations
Answering Textile Industry Critics
25. TIME IS LIMITED—MANAGE IT WELL
Water Is Limited—Manage It Well
Manage Your "Now" Time
26. WHY CORPORATE AIDS TO EDUCATION?
Why Corporate Aids to the Black Community?
Why Johnny, Jr., Can't Read
27. WISH WE'D DONE THOSE ADS
Wish I'd Taken Those Photos
Working, Not Wishing, Makes a Distributor Grow

Ice-Breakers

Audiences are like everybody else—wearing that invisible sign, "Notice me. Recognize that I'm important."

If you can work in helpful, humorous, friendly, admiring and, above all, *audience-personalized* remarks with an ice-breaker or two, your kick-off rating on a scale of 1 to 10 will shoot up to 10—a great way to start your speech.

Here are a few useful ice-breakers:

1 **Replying to Your Introducer**

(a) A simple, warmly said "thank you" always goes over well.

(b) (When your introducer has given you an especially flattering introduction.) "Thank you, Joe. (To audience)

Mark Twain said, 'I can live for two months on a good compliment.' I feel the same way about a good introduction. Wasn't that a corker? I'm going to live for two years on that one, Joe."

(c)   "Ladies and gentlemen. I always get a good introduction. I write them myself."

(d)   "Of course, ladies and gentlemen, that introduction was okay . . . a little *understated,* really . . . but Joe will learn."

2   Acknowledging a Warm Introduction and Applause

(a)   "Thank you for that warm welcome. However, I'm afraid I'm in the position now of 'The party's over. Let's begin.' Just hope I can live up to that great welcome."

(b)   "Well, thank you for that fine welcome. You know, with a welcome like that, I feel somewhat like the high-powered executive who was brought into a company as president and when asked about his financial future said, 'I shall do very well here, if *I* do very well.' So let's see if I can do very well today in telling you about . . . ."

(c)   "Thank you for that warm applause. I notice you bankers (or plumbers, retailers, etc.) can applaud better than other groups. I think it's because you have extra-strong hands. You take in so much money in your work that it develops your hands."

(d)   (Switch on the above for a community organization.) "Thank you for that fine applause. I notice you Rotarians (or other club or church group) can applaud better than other groups. I think it's because you have such big hands. You're always out there giving people a helping hand, so it develops your hands."

3   Solicitous of Audience's Comfort

Sometimes the meeting presider forgets to give the audience a seventh-inning stretch. When this happens, the savvy speaker calls one.

(a) "Let's get comfortable. Everybody stand up and stretch." (Or, "Everybody take off his coat.")

(b) "How about the pause that refreshes? Let's take 15 minutes to: (1) make a phone call—phones are on the left in the hall, (2) visit the restrooms—they're on the right in the hall. (Looking at watch) It's 10 o'clock. We'll start promptly at 10:15."

(c) "How's the air-conditioning? Would you like it turned down (up)?"

(d) (Very cold) "Hey, isn't this great air-conditioning? Who needs to go to Alaska? Now if they'd just provide us with parkas. Seriously, can someone do something about the air-conditioning?"

4 Complimenting an Audience, Organization, Neighborhood, or City

(a) "Hey, but you're a good-looking crowd. Every time I talk here you people look nicer . . . and *fresher,* too. As a matter of fact, today you look like tomorrow."

(b) Mention something the audience or organization is noted for. Example: (before a photography club) "During dinner, the president has told me of awards a number of you have won. I'm extremely impressed. I had no idea your club was doing work of this caliber."

(c) Remark on several outstanding things about the neighborhood or city. Example: "It's exciting to be in this handsome city of Albuquerque, in the state where the Atomic Age was born."

(d) Picture yourself a fan of an organization, industry, city, etc. Example: (before a group of police officers) "This is a double pleasure to talk to you today because my childhood dream of glory was to be a police officer. I couldn't pass the physical, but I assure you I seldom miss a cops-and-robbers show on TV."

5 Getting on Common Ground

Using some of the tips already mentioned, along with mentioning by name several members of the audience, can help you establish a common bond. This will insure that the start of your talk won't be blah but a blazing success.

Let's say you're a home-office executive and giving a talk in the field. Here's a rough skeleton you can use.

> (Giving name of top-ranking person in room, mentioning other important people in meeting) "and members of the (name of group), I appreciate the opportunity to talk with you today.
>
> "I suspect you know my wife (husband, sister, etc.) is a native of your fine city. It's good to be in this delightful city where (name something it's famous for).
>
> "As a member of the home team, it's nice to see those people I phone frequently or write to (look around and name them; get in as many names as you reasonably can), Bob Gillette, Alice Abrams, Larry Panelli, Boots Caldwell.
>
> "Since this is the branch that set a record for 50,000 parts last week, I have a message for the foremen, Ace Tredwell, George Link, and Helen Stanley . . . are you listening Ace, George, and Helen? I've just come from the North Dakota plant. They asked me to tell you they'll have their revenge next month.
>
> "By the way, I understand Willy Jackson has just caught a 7' fish. Willy, before I leave, I hope you'll give me a casting lesson . . ."

Building Bridges

To give a super talk, you must deftly link the points you make. The following bridges will help:

Enumerate. *Example:* Enumerate your points by saying "The first point I'd like to make . . . the second point . . ." etc. Or, "The first consideration . . . the second consideration . . ." etc. Numbering your points adds greater clarity.

Signpost. A pro speaker reinforces his numbered points or reasons by signposting. That is, he holds up one finger for the first point or reason, hoists two fingers for the second, etc.

Echoes. Often, you can make a transition from one point to another by echoing a few words. *Example:* A speaker concludes a portion of his talk with . . . "and you'll find this type of fund raising personally satisfying to do." To move to the next section of his talk, he uses a transition that echoes a few of the preceding words: "Now another satisfaction in fund raising is . . . ."

Symbols.   A speaker can make transitions in his talk by using symbols. *Example:* A speaker is talking about the use of witchcraft by Wall Street. When he wishes to move from his introduction to the use of crystal ball reading, he can hold up a crystal ball. When he wishes to move from that section to palmistry, he can hold up a drawing of a charted palm. The audience can then easily follow the course of his talk.

Word transitions. Often, phrases like, "On the other hand . . ." "Consequently . . ." "Next we'll consider . . ." "And furthermore . . ." can link parts of a talk so they can easily be grasped by listeners.

Jumping to another topic.   Sometimes a speaker has different subjects to cover. Phrases like these can help his listeners stay tuned in: "Changing to another subject . . ." "Still another challenge in a different area . . ." "At this point I suggest . . ." "Turning to another part of our program . . ."

Remember to use bridges. If you don't, you can drive your listeners straight into the cold depths of confusion.

Openers and Closers

Suppose you need a few ideas for kicking off and ending a talk. Below are some handy openers and closers. You can utilize them in various ways: (a) in their entirety, (b) mixing one opener with another closer, and (c) retailoring them to suit your situation. For example, here's how you might retailor #9 on ecology for use with a talk to industry.

The ecology opener reads: "Today I want to talk to you about conservation—how we can lift it out of a slogan into a program." To change it to an industry opener, you might recast it this way: "Today I want to talk about an industry improvement—how we can lift it out of a slogan into a program."

Also, you'll find that checking through these openers and closers will hatch ideas for possible talks.

1   Accounting

OPENER Recently, *The Wall Street Journal* quoted a business executive telling the story of how another businessman with a rather shady reputation was interviewing applicants for the job of chief accountant.

He asked two applicants: "How much are two plus two?" Both answered "four," and neither got the job. The third applicant, when asked the same question, got up, closed the door, drew the blinds, leaned across the desk and said, "How much would you like it to be?"

All joking aside, accounting today is becoming much more specialized.

CLOSER   In conclusion, I hope these things I've given you from my own experience in accounting will be helpful.

2   Advantages

OPENER   Mark Twain once said, "Everyone is a moon and has a dark side, which he never shows to anybody." A retailer (or banker, or photography bug, etc.) is a moon, too, but one with a *bright* side that he doesn't show to others too often. Tonight, however, I would like to show you something of this bright side . . . some of the advantages of being a retailer (banker, photography buff, etc.).

CLOSER   I've shown you some bright sides of my moon tonight. I hope my moon *shinings* have helped you.

3   Advertising

OPENER   Yesterday I was glancing through a newspaper and noticed an ad with a big headline that said NAGGING BACKACHE! Do you ever think they're going too far in what they're selling these days . . . BACKACHE! However, today there's another kind of advertising I'd like to talk to you about.

CLOSER   I've talked to you today about some special facets of advertising. And I'd like to conclude by describing a scene I witnessed with three little neighborhood kids. One little girl said, "Let's play house. Let's pretend we're the Roberts Family. I'll be Mama Roberts." "And I'll be Papa Roberts," said a little boy. And the third little boy spoke up and said, "I'll be the commercial."

4   Business

OPENER   Today we must mind our business of (naming type of business, banking, retailing, etc.) so we'll have some business to mind. I'd like to discuss three issues in our business:
1.   Unemployment
2.   Capitalization
3.   Inflation

(*Note:* You can substitute three pertinent issues for your business.)

CLOSER   In summing up, I feel our business can flourish because the United States still is a democracy. And as Winston Churchill said of democracy: "It is the worst system—except for all those other systems that have been tried and failed."

5   Civil Rights

OPENER   It seems to me that one of the problems of civil rights is we often forget to be *civil*. Today I'd like to talk about putting civility into action . . ."

CLOSER   Now I'm going to pass out an outline of a few steps our company has followed in emphasizing the *civil* in civil rights. I hope they'll help you as they've helped us.

6   Credit

OPENER   You know, there's a certain profile emerging with Americans today. They're giving themselves everything credit will buy. So let's talk about today's credit picture in (name of business).

CLOSER   I'd like to wind up with this reminder: Now when babies are born in hospitals, they no longer put tiny identification bracelets on them. No sir. Each baby has attached—right to his wrist—his own little credit card. Believe me, credit's big business today.

7   Crime

OPENER   Recently— and this is a true story, though I've changed the names of the kids involved—a 12-year-old named

Sharon became a sophisticated blackmailer. She set her sights on Bobby, a little boy she noticed who had plenty of candy money. She slipped him threatening and demanding messages in code. For example, when she wanted money, she counted the numbers of the alphabet and scrawled 13-15-14-5-25 for money.

Bobby got the idea all right. Especially when she'd call him up at night and tell him where to leave the pay-off. She'd include a little action message like, "If you don't pay up, I'll beat you up and I don't mean kicking or hitting—I mean bruising you and blackening your eyes."

After he'd given Sharon over $50, Bobby finally told his mother what he was going through, and she called the police. When they talked with the school principal, he said he'd had problems with Sharon in the past.

Sharon, of course, is small potatoes when it comes to crime in our cities and the nation. Today, I'd like to talk to you about some causes and solutions to crime in our city.

CLOSER   Now, in conclusion, I'll pass out a few guidelines that will tell you what measures you can take in helping solve crime problems. If each of us would take these steps, I feel people would no longer say of our city, "That town's so dangerous even the robbers travel in twos!"

8   Disadvantaged

OPENER   The past two weeks for an hour or so every day I've lived in a different world. I've put on a blindfold, joined a blind person, gone out with him and done yard work, joined him in fixing his lunch, sat at his typewriter and typed a few letters.

I've found that when looking at things from a blind person's standpoint, the world looks very different. And I feel this experience has better prepared me to give you some tips on why it will pay you to employ the blind (or, how a charitable organization can help the blind). How we can bring them into the work force, how we can bring them into the club . . . .

CLOSER   Remember, the blind are knocking at our door. Will we welcome them into the club?

(Note: You can use a version of this opening to introduce a talk to help blacks, Indians, the mentally retarded, etc.)

9   Ecology

OPENER   Today I want to talk to you about conservation—how we can lift it out of a slogan into a program.

CLOSER   And now I'd like to end with a remark that C.K. Chesterton made: "I believe in getting in hot water. It keeps you clean."

10   Education

OPENER   I'm reminded of a famous speaker's remark, "The man who is too big to learn is as big as he will ever be." So today let's talk about some aspects of learning (in this business, in a hobby, etc.).

CLOSER   I'd like to leave one thought with you (speaking about business). We must continue to learn, to earn. (Or, speaking about a hobby) What you learn as a hobby, you may someday follow as your second career. (Or, speaking about fund raising) As a business person learns to raise funds, he also learns leadership that enhances his career.

11   Government

OPENER   Comic Jay Marr once said, "One way to beat the system: Take a 'Go Now, Pay Later' trip—but don't come back."

I think a lot of us, dissatisfied with government, have thought of doing that. But since that's not practical for most of us . . . let's take a look at how we can improve the government.

CLOSER   Before saying good night, I'd like to caution you to watch your money. Don't waste it on drink, gambling, sports cars, even life's necessities. Remember, you've got a *big* government to support.

12   Management

OPENER   A fifth-century B.C. Chinese philosopher, Lao-tzu, was something of an early management expert. One of his significant conclusions was along the lines that he who takes the longest steps does not walk the fastest.

This holds true, I've found, in management. Doing the accepted things in management—taking "the longest steps"—is all right. But I find that a manager's real progress comes when he takes the time to think about a problem, to dream a while, and contemplate original solutions. Out of thought-incubation comes ideas that will let you "walk the fastest" in management. Today, I'd like to talk about some of these ideas.

CLOSER   So don't forget, close your door, put your feet up on your desk, think, and you can "walk fastest" in management.

13   Profitability

OPENER   Increased costs of doing business, tougher competition, shrinkage of inventories from pilferage, damage by other kinds of crime, changing customer preferences—all remind us that profitability doesn't occur just by adding outlets.

Today, let's look at some pointers for profitability.

CLOSER   I believe you'll find it profitable to follow these pointers.

14   Publicity

OPENER   (Holding up a toy horn and giving a few toots) Today, I'm going to talk to you about blowing your own horn . . . publicizing your business (club, cause, etc.).

CLOSER   So blow your horn about . . . publicize your business (club, cause, etc.), for, as W.S. Gilbert said, "If you wish in the world to advance—your merits you're bound to enhance; you must stir it and stump it, and blow your own trumpet, or trust me, you haven't a chance."

15   Recession

OPENER   A prosperous businessman in (naming an industry) went with his wife to a swank Madison Avenue art gallery. Their purpose was to see a new art show by an avant-garde artist. The businessman wasn't too fond of art shows so his wife was surprised to find he'd staked out one particular picture. He stared at

it, examined it from every angle, and announced he was going to
buy it.

"You are? Why?" asked his amazed wife.

"Because," replied the businessman, "it reminds me of
business today. It doesn't make sense from any angle." Well, today, the angle I want to talk to you about is . . .

CLOSER　　I admit that business today has problems. In fact,
I recently recall a prospective business owner asking an established
businessman: "Do you think I'd be nuts to start a business at this
time?" The business owner said, "You don't *have* to be nuts, but it
helps."

16　Regulation

OPENER　　Today taxpayers' money is being wasted by excessive regulation in Washington.

Let me give two examples. A Washington wit assembled, on a
ribbon of cloth, the more than 50 forms it takes to get a federal
loan on a single-family home. The ribbon stretched out to 80 feet
in length—80 feet! Here's another example. (Give one from your
own experience.)

In a period of 10 years, the volume of federal paperwork has
doubled. It now costs, literally, billions of dollars to print, fill in,
and process paperwork due to *excessive* regulation. Well, I don't
think I have to tell you about this. But what can *we* do? Here are
some thoughts . . . .

CLOSER　　Excessive paperwork is strangling America. But
we *can*, if we'll act, get rid of this strangulation. The first thing I
want you to do tomorrow is to send a letter of protest to (giving
name and address of federal regulatory body for your industry).

17　Retirement

OPENER　　The way to retire successfully is to take your
former work—your vocation—and put an "a" in front of it. In
other words, *now* make your work your avocation. If you've
worked as a (name type of business position), put your business
talent to work as an advisor to small business people (or to help

your club or church in their business matters). Here are some examples . . . .

CLOSER So in closing, think of retiring as playing magician—just taking your former vocation, adding an "a" and making your former work your avocation—and getting some new fun out of life.

18 Risk-Taking

OPENER Tonight my subject is risk-taking in business. And I'm reminded of the time the then Secretary of State William H. Seward saw an exciting opportunity. He urged the taking of what at that period was thought of as an extreme risk: the signing of the North Pacific Treaty of Purchase in Washington, on March 20, 1867, for the purchase of Alaska from Russia.

The purchase price was $7,200,000 (less than 2¢ an acre). In that era, and until the gold rush of 1898, the public referred to this purchase as "Seward's Folly" and "Seward's Icebox." For a number of years people judged the Alaska purchase as a *big, big risk!* But like many well-thought-out risks, Alaska paid off.

CLOSER In business today, we must be ready to risk people laughing at us . . our peers criticizing us . . . even risk capital . . . in order to achieve new, better, and eventually more profitable ways of doing things.

19 Safety

OPENER I once witnessed this in a garage and shop area. A woman office employee came back to the shop to summon a mechanic to the phone. Someone had left a creeper out. The woman accidentally stepped on it—and it shot out from under her. She was thrown to the cement floor—with tremendous force. They took her to the hospital. That accident shouldn't have happened. As with many accidents, it could easily have been prevented.

(*Note:* You can substitute a safety violation in your own business.)

CLOSER Maintaining safety is an alert state of mind. It's thinking about and doing the safe thing *before* an accident occurs. In summary, let me emphasize, *safety is what we can do in advance!*

20 Senior Citizens

OPENER   Did you ever realize that when you close the door on the way you made your living, you can open a door to really living?

CLOSER   And finally, here's one secret many senior citizens have found which helps them live a wonderful life. They go by the slogan, "Age is no alibi!"

21 Statistics

OPENER   Disraeli once commented, "There are three kinds of lies: lies, damned lies, and statistics." Today I'm going to tell you about statistics ... but I assure you Disraeli wouldn't have termed *these* statistics about production (mental health, alcoholism, etc.) lies. Let me show you. . . .

CLOSER   I believe you will agree with me that the statistics and facts we've looked at don't lie. And that we must indeed act now to improve production (mental health, alcoholism, etc.).

22 Support

OPENER   I have a salesman friend who, years ago, did very badly when he began to sell. In fact, we made jokes about him, like saying he couldn't sell a kitchen gadget to the world's most dedicated gourmet cook. But one day he started to turn on in selling. When I asked him why, he said, "Well, I learned one thing."

"What was that?"

"To ask for the order," he said. "When I actually asked for the order, sales turned around."

I'm not a salesman, but today I'm here to ask for the order ... ask for your support on an important matter . . . ."

CLOSER   Before I leave you today, I want to remind you to support this project by (detail how you want them to act, such as writing their congressman, taking a certain step in business, etc.).

23 Time

OPENER A management consultant has said, "We waste 35% of our business time thinking about things *that have already happened.*" No wonder we don't get as much accomplished as we'd like to. Let's talk for a few minutes on how to expand our time.

CLOSER Before I sign off, I'd like to tell you about the working habits of Anthony Trollope, a nineteenth-century novelist who wrote a lot of books. He worked for the British Post Office and wrote in his spare time.

He guarded his time and it was his practice to be at his desk at 5:30 a.m. He put his watch on his desk and made himself write for three hours, completing 250 words every 15 minutes. If he completed a book one day, he frugally started another book the next morning—without a vacation. So let's start a few books—or other tasks—when we have a spare 15 minutes.

24 Tour

OPENER (You can start with a summary or highlights of a tour, as in this tour of business branch locations.) I'm happy to have this opportunity to speak to you today . . . and to share with you the results of my recent experiences which have included visiting six factories in two weeks . . . seeing our branch in Georgia, now on three shifts to meet production . . . taking a few hours off from touring a western factory to visit one of the finest salmon streams in Oregon . . . and flying up to our Ontario factory in a little plane the pilot built himself—literally. (The speaker could also describe his findings when telling about a tour of retail outlets, a vacation spent visiting golf courses in the Carolinas, etc.)

CLOSER In closing I must say that before this trip I was like the big dog, Rupert, that I saw in my optician's shop the other day. Rupert was standing on his hind legs, pressing his nose against the letters on the eye chart. His mistress said with annoyance, "Rupert won't admit he needs glasses."

Before I took this trip, I guess I kind of resembled Rupert. I refused to admit what a great job was going on throughout our company (or, how great these golf courses are). This trip really opened my eyes and I hope sharing what I saw has opened yours, too.

25 Women

OPENER (Suitable for addressing a female audience in a field with many women employees—such as insurance, banking, teaching.) It's my observation that women do much of the real work in this field (naming it). I know it, you know it, and your bosses know it. The time has come for new score-keeping. It's time for management to recognize your contributions to this industry (or field). Let's talk for a few minutes about how women can achieve tangible recognition in their work.

CLOSER Remember, you women helped make this country a land of opportunity—now you deserve yours.

26 Work

OPENER You know, there's a lot of talk about work-aholics . . . those people who work 16 hours a day . . . who secretly *erase* their names from the vacation schedule . . . and then swear they already have taken their vacation.

Well, we may not spawn a crew of workaholics, but I think a lot of us are finding more adventure and interest in our work since (describe an improved or new system or selling method, etc.).

CLOSER You know the remark about a workaholic. "At least he's not a quitter." This new system (or selling method) will keep a lot of us from wanting to be quitters—it's got a long-range potential for us all.

27 Youth

OPENER Some years ago I hired a young person at $4.00 an hour. He was very happy to have a job and said, "You're paying me $4.00 an hour, and I'm going to give you $8 of work for every hour I put in." And frankly he did.

More than that he was a wonderer, a "what-if-er," he asked

questions. He tried hard to find new answers to puzzling problems. And he succeeded. Our company still needs that kind of worker . . . .

CLOSER   Finding these answers to puzzling problems may sound like work. Indeed, it *is* work. But let me assure you, there's no game I've ever found—and I used to play hard baseball and hockey—that is as interesting as work. I believe you'll find that's true, too.

TREASURE CHEST 2

Miracle Speaker's Reservoir of Sparkling Stories and Witty Words

In this section you'll find punch lines, anecdotes, and quotes to muscle up and spice your talk. So browse, select, enjoy.

Achievement

1 It pays to be ignorant, for when you're smart, you already know it can't be done.   —*Jeno's Credos*
2 Reaching for the stars? You may not get one, but neither will you come up with a handful of mud.
3 However diverse their talents, temperaments and differences, all great achievers have one trait in common: they never bother to look around and compare themselves with other men, but are content to run their own race on their own terms.   —*Sydney J. Harris*

4   The ideas of men like Henry Ford are ideas of
     brilliance; their implementation is genius. I am con-
     vinced that it is only the man who can both generate a
     good idea and implement it who can be called a genius.
     I have a sneaking suspicion that many of the "best"
     ideas never see the light of day. Lots of poor or at least
     limited ideas have made it, simply because they were
     picked up by some snarly overachiever who simply
     would not quit.   —*Peter H. Engel*

Action

5   Out of the strain of the doing,
     Into the peace of the done
                             —*Julia Louise Matilda Woodruff*
6   That spirit which
     Most often sings
     Belongs to people
     Doing things.   —*Paul Armstrong*
7   To wrestle with a bad feeling only pins our attention on
     it, and keeps it still fostered in the mind; whereas, if we
     act as if we feel better, the old bad feeling soon folds its
     tent and silently steals away.   —*Henry James*

Actor

8   A TV actor who was out of work decided to audition
     for the role of Abraham Lincoln in a TV drama. He
     read several biographies of Lincoln, practiced his man-
     nerisms, and rented a shawl and stovepipe hat. Looking
     in the mirror, he was delighted to find he looked exactly
     like President Lincoln. Unfortunately, on the way to the
     audition, the actor was assassinated.

Advertising

9   Many a small thing has been made large by the right
     kind of advertising.   —*Mark Twain*

10   Advertising and salesmanship are the gas and oil that fuel industry.   —*Dr. Kenneth McFarland*

11   Advertising is no game for a quitter.

                                        —*John Wanamaker*

12   Eighty-five percent of all advertising is ignored.

                                        —*Jay Taylor*

13   Madison Avenue is where they took the padding out of the shoulders and put it in the expense account.

14   Receptionist in advertising agency Bartlett, Wolf and Smith, to caller: "I'm sorry, Mr. Bartlett's retired, Mr. Wolf is out campaigning to be mayor, and Mr. Smith is being held hostage."

15   William Wrigley, the chewing gum tycoon, placed great faith in advertising. He expressed his advertising philosophy as: "Tell 'em quick—tell 'em often."

Advice

16   Advice is like snow; the softer it falls the longer it dwells upon, and the deeper it sinks into the mind.

                                        —*Samuel Taylor Coleridge*

Africa

17   Always something new out of Africa.

                                        —*Pliny the Elder*

18   The darkest thing about Africa has always been our ignorance of it.   —*George H. T. Kimble*

Age

19   I tell people I'm pushing 50. They say it looks more like I'm dragging it.   —*Jack C. Taylor*

20   On the occasion of Zsa Zsa Gabor's seventh marriage, a reader wrote a magazine to ask Zsa Zsa's age. The editor gallantly replied, "For Miss Gabor, time has stood still."

21   Benjamin Franklin remarked that all people want to live long, but no one wants to grow old.

Animals

22 The quickest way to become an old dog is to stop learning new tricks.   —*Modern Maturity*

23 Doggone rules. Sign in a hotel: "Dogs are permitted because we never had a dog who smoked in bed and burned up the sheets. Never had a dog who stole the towels. Never had a dog who got drunk and caused a ruckus. So if your dog can vouch for you, you're welcome."   —*Phillips Petroleum PHILNEWS*

24 The little boy was given a full-grown St. Bernard for his birthday. Looking at his prize with delight and wonder, he asked his daddy, "Is he mine or am I his?"
                                        —*Samuel J. Stannard*

25 "My, what a strange-looking cow," exclaimed the city dweller to the farmer. "How come it hasn't any of those big horns?"

"There are many reasons," replied the farmer quietly. "Some cows don't have them until later in life. Others have them removed, while other breeds are born without horns. That particular cow doesn't have horns because it's a horse."   —*Boys' Life*

Arabs

26 You're worried about oil? Suppose the Arabs also controlled C and D batteries!

Architecture

27 Architecture is 90% business and 10% art.
                                        —*Arthur G. Odell, Jr.*

28 I call architecture frozen music.   —*Madame de Staël*

Argument

29 "What's the shape of the earth?" asks Judy's teacher. Judy says it is round. "How do you know it's round,

Judy?" Judy replies, "All right, it's square then. I don't wanna start an argument about it."

30 Lady Bracknell: "I dislike arguments of all kinds. They are always vulgar, and often convincing."

—*Oscar Wilde*

Art

31 Painting is the art of making the invisible visible.
32 Art is either a revolutionist or a plagiarist.

—*Paul Gauguin*

Auto

33 Sales manager to car owner: "We can't take your trade, but we did get a bid from the junk dealer."
34 The trouble with cars is they don't outlive the payments.
35 An engineer has developed an alternative to warning buzzers in auto. He hooks a tape system to dashboard warning gauges. When he runs low on gasoline or fails to fasten his seat belt, his wife's voice lets him know. One tape shouts, "Your engine is overheating. I see steam. Do something." —*The Wall Street Journal*
36 Dealer to man driving away in a used car he has just bought: "If it gives you any trouble, don't let us know. We *hate* trouble."

Attack

37 My left is broken, my right is weakened; the situation is excellent. I am attacking! —*Marshall Foch*

Award

38 (After she had won her second Emmy in two years.) I felt like an orange that was just selected over an apple.

—*Mary Tyler Moore*

Banking

39 If bankers are so smart, how come they try to collect service charges from the customers with the least money in their accounts?   *—Changing Times*

40 I don't want to imply that my bank account is low, but the manager of the bank knocked on my door this morning and asked for his calendar back.
                                        —Henney Youngman

41 That town is a great banking center. All its creeks have two banks and the bullfrogs in the creeks have greenbacks.

Bible

42 The Lord my God will enlighten my darkness.
                                        —Psalms 18:28

43 A merry heart doeth good *like* a medicine: but a broken spirit drieth the bones.   *—Proverbs 17:22*

44 Seest thou a man diligent in his business? He shall stand before kings; he shall not stand before mean *men*.
                                        —Proverbs 22:29

45 *There is* a path which no fowl knoweth, and which the vulture's eye hath not seen.   *—Job 28:7*

Birthday

46 New Year's Day is every man's birthday.
                                        —Charles Lamb

47 Little kid, with finger on switch of an electric fan beside a big cake covered with candles, says: "Make a wish, Dad. I'll see that you get it."

48 Husband to guest at wife's birthday party: "How old is my wife? I don't really know. When we married, we were the same age. Now, she's much younger than I am."

Borrowed

49 The way we figger, a friend in need can be a pest indeed.
—Herb. Daniels

Brains

50 An ounce of patience is worth a pound of brains.
51 I not only use all the brains I have but all I can borrow.
—Woodrow Wilson
52 Your body is about 65% water. Your brain cells are 70% water.
—Harper's Bazaar

Brotherhood

53 You don't live in a world all alone. Your brothers are here, too.
—Albert Schweitzer
54 Until you have become really, in actual fact, a brother to everyone, brotherhood will not come to pass.
—Dostoevski

Business

55 Business is the greatest game I know.
—Willard F. Rockwell, Jr.
56 It's almost as difficult to divest yourself of a business empire as to build one.
57 (Business manager) He's like an alarm clock. He wakes people up.
58 Coming together is a beginning
Keeping together is progress
Working together is success.
—Henry Ford II
59 When a new employee asked Thomas Edison what the rules of the laboratory were, Edison said, "Hell, there ain't no rules here. We're trying to accomplish somep'n!"

60 It isn't the business you get; it's the business you hold
    that counts.

61 Management experts Herbert and Jeanne Greenberg,
    who operate the Marketing Survey & Research Corp.,
    studied the personnel of 7,000 corporations. They found
    80% of employees were in the wrong jobs. Why?
    Because they were hired for education, age, experience,
    race, and sex and not for what the management experts
    find really counts—personality.

62 A foreman was asked by a young worker: "Does com-
    pany loyalty mean only that I give a fair day's work for
    a fair day's pay?"
        The foreman said, "That's not all it means. The
    company's side of loyalty also means a *good* day's pay
    for a *good* day's work."

Cause

63 The causes of things are ever more interesting than the
    events themselves.   —*Cicero*

64 Happy the man who has been able to understand the
    causes of things.   —*Virgil*

Children

65 Small children, small joys; big children, big annoys.
                                        —*Yiddish Proverb*

66 An ounce of child care is worth more than a pound of
    child cure.

67 Insanity is hereditary. You can catch it from your kids.

68 The marble tournament was in full swing. One little boy
    missed an easy shot and let a real cuss word slip.
        "Edward!" called the preacher from the spectators'
    bench, "What do little boys who swear when they're
    playing marbles turn into?"
        "Golfers," was the reply.   —*Jobber Topics*

69 Tradition has it that a small boy was once asked if he
    could play the violin. "I expect so," he replied. "I've
    never tried."

70   My Cub Scouts had a happy summer learning about birds and animals, but now school was starting so I suggested to my son that a haircut would be in order. His protest had validity in the animal world.

    "But Mom," he said. "I'm just going into my animal phase, and I need all the hair I can grow."

                                     —Patricia Paden

71   Actually I have no rapport with kids. I was in Florida last week. I sent my nephew two baby alligators. He threw them in a blender and tried to make Gatorade. One time I gave him an ant farm. He hired an anteater to manage it.   *—Ed Bluestone*

72   A father was explaining to his first grader where Rhode Island was. "It's just above New York," he said. There was a pause. "Daddy do you mean the world has two stories?"   *—Ina Hughs*

Children (Voting)

73   Why not give children voting rights? Perhaps American kids 8 to 13 inclusive could each receive 1/4 vote; 14-17 inclusive, 1/2 vote; and 18-20 inclusive, 3/4 vote. Voting youngsters would be (1) more interested in the democratic system and (2) call political attention to themselves and their needs.

Coaching

74   I'd define coaching as the job of getting men to play up to the best of their natural resources.   *—Fritz Crisler*

Collection

75   And now, brethren, let us give in accordance with what we reported on Form 1040.

Communism

76   Give me four years to teach the children, and the seed I
have sown will never be uprooted.   —*Lenin*

Competition

77   There is no better way to get ahead of your competition
than when he is pessimistic and entrenched in preserving his old ways.   —*Frank Butrick*

Conformity

78   A man flattened by an opponent can get up again. A
man flattened by conformity stays down for good.
—*Thomas J. Watson, Jr.*

Conscience

79   Conscience is the small inner voice that warns us
somebody may be looking.   —*H. L. Mencken*

Conservative

80   We're often conservative in the U.S. because there's so
much to conserve.

Consumerism

81   A senior vice-president of a utility company, plagued by
complaints from consumers and environmentalists,
says: "I sleep like a baby—sleep two hours then wake
up and cry."
82   (Closer for a radio program of tips for shoppers) They'll
make you skilled in the art of *shelf* defense.
83   It disturbs me that the consumer has become increasingly distrustful of the businesses she deals with. The

word "rip-off" has become almost a catechism. She doesn't trust the supermarket. She doesn't trust advertising. She doesn't trust business. Communicating reasonably with the consumer has become increasingly difficult.

—Ira C. Herbert

Contentment

84 According to Dr. Louis Binstock, Grandpa Tubbs, who'd been stubborn and crabby for years, suddenly became sweetness and light. When asked what caused the change, he replied, "Well, sir, I've been striving all my life for a contented mind. It's done no good. So I've just decided to be contented without it."

—Og Mandino

Conversation

85 Superior people talk about ideas, mediocre people talk about things, little people talk about other people.

86 We often repent of what we have said, but never, never, of that which we have not.   *—Thomas Jefferson*

87 Then there was the absent-minded business correspondent who kept forgetting to complete his . . . .

Cost of Living

88 The cost of living hasn't affected its popularity.

—John D. Yeck

89 The man who said the best things in life are free had a great sense of humor.   *—Altman's ad*

Courage

90 Courage is not the absence of fear, it is the conquest of it.   *—Frank Bettger*

91 My philosophy has been that, regardless of the circum-
stances, I shall not be vanquished, but will try to be happy. Life . . . is a continual challenge, and it is up to us to
be cheerful—and to be strong, so that those who depend
on us may draw strength from our example.
                                              —*Rose Kennedy*

92 Never let your head hang down. Never give up and sit
down and grieve. Find another way.
                                        —*Leroy (Satchel) Paige*

Courtesy

93 Of courtesy, it is much less
Than courage of heart, or holiness;
Yet in my heart it seems to me
The grace of God is in courtesy.   —*Hillaire Belloc*

Creativity

94 One part of a business person must know how to create
ideas; the other part must know how to sell them.

95 Business men who devise new methods, new processes,
new ways of working, new organizations of men and
materials, men who visualize new projects, new plans,
new developments, or entire new industries, do as much
original thinking as the keenest poet or inventor.
                                              —*Daniel Starch*

96 Doctor F.L. Wells once made a study of two groups.
One consisted of men receiving average salaries, the
other of men receiving superior salaries. In tests of in-
telligence, both groups ranked about equal. They dif-
fered in one respect. The higher-salaried men were
more creative. They could think up more ideas and
visualize more methods for putting them into effect.
                                              —*Dora Albert*

Credit

97 To man applying for a car loan: "For your convenience I'm having the payment schedule engraved on the windshield."

98 No man can take full credit for everything he has done.

Crime

99 A robber returning to Sing Sing for the third time was asked why he continued to hold up banks. He answered, "Because that's where the money is."

Charles F. Adams

100 "How could you swindle people who trusted you?" asked the judge. Replied the man: "Your honor, it's almost impossible to swindle people who don't trust you."   —*New York State Vegetable Growers News*

101 As the bank robbers finished their work they noticed the gagged cashier frantically indicating a desire to talk. After loosening the gag he pleaded, "Take the books, too. I'm $4000 short."   —*Parts Pup*

102 Perhaps one way to keep youth from criminal acts is offering employment such as Holland offered. One year when half of Holland's unemployed were under 23 years of age, the Dutch government took innovative employment steps. In essence the plan called for "duo-jobs," whereby two youths would be hired for each vacant position. Each youth got half the wages and half the unemployment compensation, which is about 80% of the full wage in Holland. Employers also receive funds from the government for setting up new jobs.

Critic

103 If you don't want to be criticized, say nothing, do nothing, be nothing.

104 Be your own best critic.

Cynic

105   What is a cynic? A man who knows the price of
       everything but the value of nothing.   —*Oscar Wilde*

Debate

106   (Speaking about a free press) Debate—boisterous
       debate—is the lifeblood of a free society.
                              —*Arthur Ochs Sulzberger*

Demonstration

107   One demonstration is worth more than a thousand
       words.   —*Frank Bettger*

Dentist

108   Patient: "What do you charge for pulling a tooth?"
       Dentist: "$25."
       Patient: "What! For only two seconds of work?"
       Dentist: "Well, if you wish, I can pull it very slowly."

Desire

109   You can get what you desire and in just the measure of
       that desire.   —*Thomas Dreier*

Diet

110   I just got back from a "fat farm." That's where they
       make molehills out of mountains.   —*Leona Toppel*
111   Ever tried the sweet potato diet? It's great! You can eat
       as many sweet potatoes as you like. You'll lose six
       pounds a week, as long as you keep moving so as not to
       root.

Divorce

112   If we did get a divorce, the only way he [my husband]
      would know it is if they would announce it on Wide
      World of Sports.   —*Dr. Joyce Brothers*

Doctor

113   Nurse talking to patient on the telephone: "Yes, the
      doctor will consider a house call. What time can you be
      at his house?"   —*The Lion*

Dress

114   I have a lot of trouble getting my husband to buy
      clothes. His idea of a dinner jacket is carrying
      sandwiches in his pocket.   —*Dana Lorge*

Driving

115   Sign in a parking lot: "Drive with fender-loving care."
                                    —*Open Road Magazine*
116   Truck driver upon being cited for 40 years of safe driv-
      ing: "I've found that the critical area is the six inches
      between the ears of each driver."
117   A male motorist waited patiently for the lady driver in
      front of him to drive onto the expressway where there
      was a "Yield Right of Way" sign. Finally his patience
      was exhausted and he yelled, "Lady, read the sign,
      please. It says 'Yield,' not 'Give up.' "—*Anne Dirkman*

Ease

118   Great man is completely at ease. Petty man is always on
      edge.   —*Confucius*

Ecology

119   Chip: "What are all the ropes around those trees for?"
Woody: "Those aren't ropes, they're flea collars."
Chip: "You mean—"
Woody: "Yes, this is a grove of dogwood."
—*Alec Buchan*

Education

120   The wildest colts make the best horses, if they only get
properly trained and broken in.   —*Themistocles*
121   Father to mother: "At least this report card proves he
isn't taking any mind-expanding drugs."
—*Today's Chuckle*
122   Some 7000 privately owned trade and technical schools
offer 550 different courses to about 2,000,000 students
each year. Courses last from a few weeks to three years,
with tuition ranging from $200 to $1800 per course.
There is a course offered somewhere for almost every
type of job.   —*Muriel Lederer*

Emotion

123   When a guy blows his top, it's constructive criticism.
When a woman does, she's emotionally unstable.
—*Woody Woodbury*

Employment

124   "How long have you been working for this company?"
"Ever since the boss threatened to fire me."
—*Lucille S. Harper*
125   Do you want a job—or a career? It's up to you.
Someone has to give you a job. If a job, it belongs to
your employer and he can give it to someone else
whenever he wants to. If a career, it's yours and
although you may have an employer, he can't give your
career to anyone else.   —*Aline Thompson*

126 Personnel director: "I've noticed that everyone, after he's been in a job awhile, tailors it to fit his own aptitudes. Gradually, he takes on the kind of tasks he does best and finds ways to get out of doing what he doesn't like to do. That's why we constantly have to write new job descriptions."
—Aline Thompson

Entertainment

127 The greatest art is entertainment. Love, joy and entertainment are always present in great art.
—Charles Lloyd

128 What entertains, interests, diverts or amuses one person may be indescribably boring to another.

129 To be entertaining, always keep a little in reserve. Don't tell everything you know—at least not all at once. Keep 'em coming back—to read the next chapter or hear what comes next.

Europe

130 Must every little language have a country.
—Jerome Frank

131 The situation in Germany is serious but not hopeless; the situation in Austria is hopeless but not serious.
—Viennese saying

Execution

132 I am mine own executioner.　　　*—John Donne*

Executive

133 Part of an executive's job is encouraging people to think and act.

134 When people comment that a man is a born executive, they really mean that his father owns the business.
—Today's Chuckle

135   I got the handle on this executive kind of early. We were walking down the street several years ago and I remarked it was a beautiful day. He answered, "Thank you."

136   The new chairman of the board said, "Now let it be understood the day of the yes-man is over. Everybody agree?"

137   Part of an executive's job is to decide what he's not going to do. Good executives are experts on what to neglect.

138   (When notifying an executive of a promotion) George, you seem too surprised to be surprised.

Exercise

139   Why is it a businessman will go from his air-conditioned home to his air-conditioned office in his air-conditioned car, then go to a health club and pay $50 an hour to sweat?   —*Tommy Moore*

140   You can exercise a lot of things besides your body, you know. You can exercise restraint in eating, drinking, and smoking, for example. You can also exercise your right to be different, to be happy. You can, in short, devise many types of exercises that will improve the quality of your life.

Experience

141   After all, experience is the name we all give to our mistakes.

Family

142   Joan Rivers doesn't think her parents appreciated her when she was a kid. "On Halloween," she recalls, "they used to send me out as is."   —*Bennett Cerf*

143   Education psychologist Jung Bay Ra made a study of the effects of television on children and families. She

asked 156 children, ages 4-6: "Which do you like better, TV or daddy?" Almost half the children said TV. Mothers fared better, with 80 percent of the children favoring moms to TV.

144   The head of a family may be of either sex. If the husband and father is boss, it is no doubt an old-fashioned family.

If the wife and mother is boss, it is a well-organized family.

If neither is boss, it is a very modern family and kids sit at the head of the table—whenever they are home.
—*Carl Riblet, Jr.*

Family Business

145   When you run a family business, the shareholders don't wait for a meeting to tell you how to run the company.
—*Charles E. Hayworth*

Fishing

146   On our Klamath River the sturgeon run to 200 pounds. One time a city dude hooked into one of these brutes and played it for hours with no success. Finally his guide slipped off his clothes and dived into the water, following the fishing line to the bottom. He found an old junked car down there and the sturgeon was inside it. The guide tried to get behind the big fish and work him out so the dude could reel him in. But every time he got close, the critter would roll up the car window.
—*Bob Steele*

147   A fishing buff asked an advertising agency account executive, who constantly talked "production-wise," "gross national product-wise," and "rating-wise," how to fish a certain stream in the New Hampshire White Mountains. He received a four-word note in reply: "Advise dries-flies-wise."

Freedom

148 The free man is he who does not fear to go to the end of
his thought.   —*Leon Blum*

149 No person can be said to enjoy civil liberty who has no
share in legislation, and no person is secure in society
unless the laws are known and respected.
—*Noah Webster*

Friend

150 A friend is a present you give yourself.
—*Robert Louis Stevenson*

151 Do you know who my best friend is? My wife.
—*Tony Randall*

152 A good friend is someone who knows all about you but
likes you anyway.

153 If you want to make an enemy your friend, let him do
you a favor.

154 Lonely? Just look around you for someone who needs a
friend, be that friend and you have a friend.

155 Friendship is the only cement that will ever hold the
world together.   —*Woodrow Wilson*

Future

156 I believe that man will not only endure: he will prevail.
—*William Faulkner*

157 Don't worry *only* about robberies and house-breakings
increasing. In the future, it's predicted that minds, and
not just houses, will be broken into and entered.

158 *In the year 2000* fifteen experts predict: College students
will make "field trips" to other planets; fewer personal
cars and more personal helicopters; a decentralized, less
powerful federal government; free medical care for
everyone; three-to-four day work weeks and six-month
vacations.   —*The National Enquirer*

Gift

159   Every gift, though it be small, is in reality great if it is given with affection.   *—Pindar*

Goal

160   If a man does not know to what port he is steering, no wind is favorable to him.   *—Seneca*

Golf

161   Wife to husband at front door carrying golf clubs, "You don't have to go all the way to the golf course for a hole in one. There's one in the roof, one in the screen door, one in the ....   *—Bob Barnes*

162   A guy is taking his first golf lesson and he asks the golf pro, "Well, what do I do?"

The pro points to the hole 400 yards away and says, "Hit this little white ball as far down the fairway as you can."

The guy proceeds to hit the ball 398 yards, two yards from the cup. The golf pro gives him a funny look, and they get in the cart and drive down to the ball.

Then the guy asks the pro, "What do I do now?"

The pro says, "Well, now you put that little ball in that little cup over there."

The guy says, "Why didn't you tell me that when we were back there?"   *—Rick Starr*

Government

163   Since I have not been employed as an official, I know how to do things.   *—Confucius*

164   It is hard to find a man who will study for three years without thinking of a post in government.*—Confucius*

165   I am still going to fight for the liberty of the citizens of the United States to make foolish decisions by themselves, rather than having wise decisions made for them by the most benevolent bureaucrat.

   —Sam J. Ervin, Jr.

166   Even though Congress passed a law regulating warranties, there's no guarantee it will work.
                                                      —*Changing Times*

167   The aggregate happiness of society . . . is, or ought to be, the end of all government.   —*George Washington*

168   Speaking of taxes, one observer notes that in the Dark Ages feudal serfs had to work three months out of every year for their masters. Today the average American works four months of the year for his government.

Government Program

169   I don't deny that there are inequities. In a [government economic] program of this sweep and magnitude, I'd be amazed if there weren't. But there are anough inequities to go around.   —*Lee A. Iacocca*

Government Spending

170   The government paid out $11 million one recent year to beekeepers whose honeybees were killed by pesticides sprayed on neighbors' property—and another $46,100 to study "environmental determinants of human aggression."   —*Lucia Mouat*

Growth

171   Democracy cannot be sustained unless you have growth in the economy that sustains the democracy. You've got to have growth or you will have a disquieted labor force and that means trouble, trouble, trouble . . . .
                                    —*Lord Rhodes, Baron of Saddleworth*

172   When you cease to be better, you'll cease to be any good.

173   Harmony makes small things grow; lack of it makes great things decay.   —*Sallust*

Guidelines

174 Tell him to live by yes and no—yes to everything good and no to everything bad. —*William James*

Guns

175 Guns and teen-agers don't mix. In fact, I hate to see gun shops running "back to school" sales.

176 Be not afraid of any man, no matter what his size. When danger threatens, call on me. I will equalize.
    —*Inscription on a revolver barrel*

177 I believe the time has come to disarm, the time to cast away personal weapons of death, the time to reduce the level of violence and carnage with handguns.
    —*Maynard Jackson*

Happiness

178 Happiness is the art of making a bouquet of those flowers within reach.

Hatred

179 Carlyle, the great writer, was once walking down the street with a companion. As they passed another man, Carlyle muttered, "I hate that man." His companion replied, "I didn't realize you knew him." Carlyle responded, "I don't know him. That's why I hate him."

Hero

180 To believe in the heroic makes heroes. —*Disraeli*

Holidays

181 Christmas is what we have 40 shopping days until, and Washington's Birthday is mostly the date when new cars are unveiled in automobile showrooms.
    —*Melvin Maddocks*

Hunting

182   Bore: "That rug on the floor is from a bear I shot in the wilds out west. It was a case of him or me."
Bored: "Have to admit—the bear certainly makes a better rug." —*George Bergman*

183   A hunter couldn't make his call work properly because he had a cold. A desperate need to blow his nose produced a loud honk and a 19-pound wild turkey gobbler responded. Two more toots on the schnozz and the bird walked into full view. —*Jim Bashline*

Hurry

184   The hurrieder I go the behinder I get.
—*Pennsylvania Dutch saying*

Hurts

185   Some of your hurts you have cured,
And the sharpest you still have survived,
But what torments of grief you endured
From evils which never arrived! —*Emerson*

Idea

186   When you get an idea, you've got to think of a reason for doing it, not of a reason for not doing it.
—*Charles Kemmans Wilson*

187   Ideas control the world. —*James A. Garfield*

Illness

188   An overworked executive came down with a severe summer cold. First his voice became slightly hoarse, then extremely hoarse. Finally it gave out completely. To show he had not lost his sense of humor, he placed a sign on his desk that read, "Sorry folks. Sound is out."
One of his associates, after regarding his miserable and haggard look, placed a second sign beside the first: "Picture is terrible, too." —*Lane Olinghouse*

189   Recipe for keeping healthy? Edgar Bergen feels laughter and light-heartedness help. He quips, "It's the surly bird that catches the germ."

Imitation

190   They copied all they could follow, but they couldn't copy my mind.
And I left'em sweating and stealing, a year and a half behind.   *—Rudyard Kipling*

Income

191   I always live by this code: You can't have bread—and loaf.   *—Louis Armstrong*

192   ... the top 5% [of the population] get only 14% of all income. Even if we took all its surplus income and gave it to the working class, this would not be enough to bring the working class to parity with the middle class. And this still leaves us with the lowest class, condemned to live on 5% of the nation's income.
    —Robert L. Heilbroner

193   Today a good carpenter can make more than the average accountant.   *—Jeffrey Feinman*

Individuality

194   I swear nothing is good to me now that ignores individuality.   *—Walt Whitman*

Innovation

195   To be a success in business: be dependable, be dogged, and *be different.*

Interesting

196   Being interested makes one interesting.
    —Dr. Erich Fromm

Investment

197 I certainly didn't have much money to start with. I remember my father saying: "Don't be a hog. Pigs get fat but hogs get slaughtered." —*John D. MacArthur*

198 The game of professional investment is intolerably boring and over-exacting to anyone who is entirely exempt from the gambling instinct, whilst he who has it must pay to this propensity the appropriate toll.
—*John Maynard Keynes*

Knowledge

199 Knowledge and timber should not be much used until they are seasoned. —*Oliver Wendell Holmes*

Ladder Climbing

200 You can't climb the ladder of success with your hands in your pockets.

201 The art of using moderate abilities to advantage often brings greater results than actual brilliance.
—*La Rochefoucauld*

202 If your objective is to get your head above the pack and be seen, one way is to work like hell.
—*Arthur M. Louis*

203 Lawyers are men trained in the art of proving that white is black and black is white, depending on who pays them.

204 A little lady being examined for jury duty in a small town was asked if she knew the defense lawyer. "Yes," she snapped, "He's a crook."

"And the plaintiff's lawyer?"

"Yes, he's a crook, too."

The judge called a conference of both lawyers. "Don't ask her if she knows me or I'll fine you," he said. —*Max F. Harris*

Leadership

205   Try leadership. Detect something that should be done before others note it. Persuade others to try this step. If you have more successes than failures, that's good leadership.

206   The art of leadership is a serious matter. One must not lag behind a movement, because to do so is to become isolated from the masses. But one must not rush ahead, for to rush ahead is to lose contact with the masses. He who wishes to lead a movement must conduct a fight on two fronts—against those who lag behind and those who rush ahead.   *—Josef Stalin*

207   Leadership: A cross between playing the horses and practicing psychiatry without a license.

208   The ability to lead others is the single most important trait a businessman can possess.   *—Henry Ford*

Learning

209   Learning is acquired by reading books, but the much more necessary learning, the knowledge of the world, is only to be acquired by reading men and studying all the various editions of them.   *—Lord Chesterfield*

Leisure

210   People who do not enjoy their work seldom enjoy their leisure.   *—Farmer's Digest*

Letters

211   One survey shows over 8 million people write letters to American newspapers every year. The *New York Times* averages 40,000 of this total, but prints only 2800, or seven out of every 100 received.

Liberal

212   A liberal is one who has both feet firmly planted in the
      air.

Management

213   To get the best performance from your executive team,
      you have to orchestrate them, getting each to give his
      best and helping them to blend their strengths for peak
      performances as a group.
                                —*Stuart Atkins and Allan Katcher*
214   Recipe for management:
      • Think big
      • Set our sights on the future
      • Plan carefully
      • Keep faith with our fellow man
      • Act decisively   —*Clarence Francis*
215   The basic resources with which the manager works are
      the five M's: *M* oney, *M* aterial, *M* achinery, *M* ethods,
      M anpower.   —*Dale Carnegie & Associates*

Marital

216   Husband is watching a baseball game. Wife comes in
      looking as though she's been in a wreck. Husband:
      "Good heavens Esther, tell me what happened—just as
      soon as the game is over!"   —*Parade cartoon*
217   "The word 'conservative' doesn't apply to my hus-
      band," the admiring wife said to the poll-taker, "if you
      mean 'stuffy' or 'never take chances.' He'll take a pru-
      dent risk, but you can be assured that the risk will be
      very carefully thought out before he takes it."
218   A woman asked her husband: "What would you like for
      breakfast, darling?"
      He replied: "I'd like two eggs and toast."

"How do you want your eggs cooked?" asked his wife.

"One poached and one scrambled," he said.

The wife served his breakfast—one egg poached, one scrambled.

The husband looked at them and said, "You've done it again! You scrambled the wrong egg!"

—Cleo Lawrence

219 Being married is like an incurable illness . . . you have to chop it off to get well.   *—Christina Onassis*

220 Woman sitting at breakfast with her husband who was reading a newspaper. She says, "I didn't say anything . . . that was yesterday."

—Modern Maturity cartoon

221 Say you that I one day may be fitted with a husband? Not till God make men of some other metal than earth.

—Beatrice,
in Shakespeare's "Much Ado About Nothing"

222 A young man announced to a coworker that he was getting married. "I'm sick and tired of eating TV dinners, darning my own socks, making the bed, and going to the laundromat," he said.

"That's funny, " declared his crony. "I got divorced for the same reason."   *—Honey Green*

223 Bigamy doesn't pay. You get two mothers-in-law.

224 I never could see why they call them unhappy marriages. All marriages are happy. It's just the life afterward—budgeting, diapering the babies, listening to each others' jokes—that is unhappy.

225 If thou wouldst marry wisely marry thine equal.

—Ovid

226 Being in love with my husband means alway having nose prints on my glasses.

227 This year with Dick (my husband) makes me wish I'd been married since I was born.

—Doris Kearns Goodwin

Media

228   Grandpa says he thinks we were much better off when the media was something that thudded on your front porch each morning around six and was called a newspaper.   —*Edward Stephenson*

Mediocrity

229   I think mediocrity is one of the cardinal sins of the world.   —*Martha Graham*

Memory

230   I used to have trouble remembering names till I took that Sam Carnegie course.   —*Jack C. Taylor*

231   "Doctor, my memory is shot. I can't remember a thing."
      "How long have you had this problem?"
      "What problem?"   —*Dr. Mark L. Stein*

Microphone

232   (To illustrate a speaker's problem using a microphone)
      The story concerns the British pilot landing his plane at an American airfield in bad weather.
      Tower operator (blowing into his microphone): "Spitfire One, Spitfire One, this is Control Tower. Over."
      British pilot (fighting to control his plane): "Tower, this is Spitfire One. I say, old boy, if you're not going to kiss me, please stop blowing in my ear."
                                              —*Dr. Jerry Tarver*

Mind

233   The smaller the mind, the more interested it is in contemplating the extraordinary. The larger the mind, the more interested it is in examining the obvious.
                                              —*Sydney J. Harris*

Minorities

234   I have found that to make a contented slave, it is necessary to make a thoughtless one. —*Frederick Douglass*

235   Not the least of the black mother's talents has been that of stretching inadequate income into a livable budget. Consumer purchase studies have shown that, contrary to the usual expectation, blacks consistently balance their budgets better than whites in the same income group.   —*James Farmer*

236   A black GM executive working in minority hiring programs recalls serving on a panel and finding himself faced with five American Indian Ph.D.s. They ranged from age 60 down to a young professor. The discussion between the generations became heated when an older man talked about the Indians' regard for tradition, their ancestral culture, and how the young didn't often drift from tribal paths very far, etc., and that these things distinguished Indians from blacks.

The young professor could contain himself no longer and shouted at his elder: "You don't know what you're talking about . . . you're just an old Uncle Tomahawk!"
                                    —*Ward's Auto World*

Misfortune

237   We all have strength to endure the misfortunes of others.

Mistake

238   A man should never be ashamed to own he has been in the wrong, which is but saying, in other words, that he is wiser today than he was yesterday.

Money

239   It wasn't until I tasted money in selling that I began to enjoy working.

240   Husband: "After taking my wife and daughter on an expensive vacation trip to Paris, as we were leaving the city, my daughter blew a kiss in the direction of the Louvre and said, 'Goodbye, Louvre,' and my wife waved at the Eiffel Tower and said, 'Goodbye, Eiffel Tower,' I couldn't resist patting my slim wallet and adding, 'Goodbye, money.' "

241   If you can count your money, you don't have a billion dollars.
                                                    —*J. Paul Getty*

242   When Sam Goldwyn and George Bernard Shaw met to discuss making a film, Goldwyn spoke of his admiration for Shaw's artistic work and the *aesthetics* of filmmaking, when Shaw interrupted. "Mr. Goldwyn, the difficulty is that you care only about art, and I am interested only in money."

Motivation

243   I'm highly motivated. My boss motivated me. He threatened to fire me if I didn't produce.

Music

244   You know what happens to old fiddlers, don't you? They just fake away.
                                                    —*Isaac Stern*

Negotiating

245   All great alterations in human affairs are produced by compromise.
                                                    —*Sydney Smith*

Nostalgia

246   Nostalgia is recalling the fun without reliving the pain.

Objection

247   Nothing ever will be attempted if all possible objections must be first overcome.   *—Samuel Johnson*

Opening

248   There is the actress who shows up at premieres, screenings, receptions, teas, and charity cocktail parties. The joke is that she would attend the opening of an envelope.

249   Strange how life gives us opportunities when we least expect them! The successful manager will grasp them and prosper. The doubtful will knuckle under. It's not a crisis of our making, but its solution may turn you into a hero in your area, not only to your customers but your banker as well!   *—Marcia Miller*

250   An optimist is one who sees opportunity in every difficulty. A pessimist is one who sees difficulty in every opportunity.

Orphans

251   People are nuts. They adopt orphans. It's bad luck to have an orphan in your house. Look, he became an orphan once, he may do it again.   *—Ed Bluestone*

Parents

252   West African proverb: If a man beats a child with his right hand, he should draw the child to him with his left.

Patent

253   More than 100,000 applications are filed yearly with the U.S. Patent and Trademark Office, but only 70,000 are approved.

Patience

254   Message embroidered on a pillow in the office of Wiley-
T. Buchanan, U.S. Ambassador to Austria:
GOD GIVE ME
PATIENCE
AND I WANT IT
RIGHT *NOW!*
                                          —*Bill Quinn*

Peace

255   There must be, not a balance of power, but a community of power; not organized rivalries, but an
organized common peace.   —*Woodrow Wilson*

Pessimist

256   Definition of a pessimist: One who has had dealings
with an optimist.

Plan

257   Plan ahead to get ahead.
258   We had a plan that we followed, and it all worked out
like popcorn.   —*John Travolta*

Political

259   *(Of a politician)* He's an open book ... written in
Chinese.
260   When Gerald Ford was elected vice-president of the
United States, he told the Grocery Manufacturers of
America he felt an affinity with processors of instant
coffee, instant tea and instant oatmeal.

"This," said Ford, "is because I happen to be the nation's first instant vice-president."

And he added, "I only hope that I prove to be as pure, as digestible and as appetizing to consumers who did not have a chance to shop around for other brands of vice-presidents when I was put on the market."

—Speech at White Sulphur Springs, WV

Pollution

261 (*A feature story described jogging by John C. Sawhill, president of New York University.*) Every morning at 7:30 he runs around Washington Square Park. Then he moves quickly through the park picking up newspapers and other trash littering the area. His enthusiasm for cleaning up the park has spread to the point where other faculty, students, and staff do the same. The park has never looked so nice. *—Ron Scherer*

262 With 200,000,000 people America has something like 200,000,000 automobiles from which the pollution is appalling. But would you prefer pollution by 200,000,000 horses and the resultant horseflies?

—Oren Arnold

263 An old-timer is one who can remember when "Smoke Gets in Your Eyes" was a song and not a weather report. *—The Lion*

Practice

264 Practice is the best of all instructors.

265 A teen-ager, dressed in jeans, sweatshirt, and carrying a baseball glove, lost on a Chicago El platform asked a passer-by, "How do I get to Wrigley Field?"

The businessman regarded him thoughtfully and advised, "Practice! Practice!"

Prayer

266 Thanks to the Teacher, of me and of all, the Upholder, the Healthgiver; thanks and lowliest wondering acknowledgment.   —*Emerson*

267 Father, help us to conserve our resources and to use them for the health and healing of the nations. Amen.
—*The Prayer*

268 Off the coast of California, where I live, a woman fell into the cold Pacific at night, and in her terror screamed "HELP ME!" He did. She was able to swim for hours and reach shore. Exhausted, she gasped out, "Thank you." Four words. You don't need to be a Billy Graham or a Norman Peale to approach the throne.
—*Oren Arnold*

Prejudice

269 To be prejudiced is to be always weak.
—*Samuel Johnson*

Pressure

270 When the night is darkest, the stars come out. The kite that children play with flies higher and higher as the wind grows *stronger*. Diamonds are made under *pressure*. The large impressive oaks we admire in nature grow strong under contrary winds, and the bells that ring on Sunday were once molded through direct contact with the *hottest* flames.   —*Marc Engeler*

Product

271 (*President, interrupting phone call to ask secretary*) Someone has complained about our product. You don't happen to know what we make, do you, Miss Hopkins?
—*Punch*

272 Young housewife: "This milk—is it fresh?"
Grocer: "Fresh? Why, three hours ago it was grass!"

Profit

273   Profit is earned only in the last five minutes and 24 seconds of each hour an employee puts in on the job, according to Chicago contractor Bruno Movrich. The first and largest part of an hour—33 minutes and 45 seconds—goes to pay for an employee's wages. The next two minutes and 39 seconds pay for fringe benefits. It then takes 10 minutes and 55 seconds more to pay for overhead. Job expense (cost of materials, etc.) accounts for the next seven minutes and 17 seconds, leaving only the remaining five minutes and 24 seconds of time in which to earn a profit.

—American Painting Contractor

274   The head of an advertising agency once asked his vice-presidents to describe the aim of the company. The answer was never in doubt—to produce the best ads in the business. "Wrong," said the agency head, "The number one aim is to make money. Aim number two is to make more money. Likewise, aim number three."

—Forbes promotional letter

275   Many receive advice, few profit by it.

—Publius Syrus

Profit-sharing

276   Under profit-sharing, you penalize the able by holding on to the inept.   *—Robert Townsend*

Public Relations

277   Public relations should really be called public information.

278   Thirty years ago, there were fewer than 125 U.S. companies with formal public relations departments. Today there are tens of thousands, and the number of public relations counseling firms exceeds 2000 in the U.S. alone.   *—Denny Griswold*

Publicity

279 Lady Godiva, one of the earliest and boldest of
publicity representatives, had an easy task; all she had
to do was to present the bare facts and win her case.
—*Herbert Jacobs*

Punishment

280 Judge, passing sentence on a man: "I sentence you to
life in prison. Have a happy day."
—*Saturday Evening Post cartoon*

Raise

281 (Message in a pay envelope) This is notification you'll
receive a significant raise. The raise is to become effective when you do.

Reading

282 I've been reading more and enjoying it less.
—*John F. Kennedy*

283 He who does not read good books has no advantage
over the man who cannot read.
—*U.S. Tobacco Journal cartoon*

Real Estate

284 *(On real estate investment)*
Many of those projects seemed to be based on the
"greater fool" theory of investment, that is, even if you
foolishly pay too much for a piece of property,
sometime in the future you will be able to sell it at an
even higher price to an even greater fool.
—*Robert E. Barnett*

Recession

285   Things are tough. Ten percent of the people are on welfare, 30 percent on unemployment and the rest on sedatives.   —*Jay Marr*

286   The president's top economic braintruster says the recession has run its course, but unemployment will remain high. I read this to mean: The depression is over for everybody but people.   —*James L. Trichon*

287   "How's business?" an 80-year-old veteran car dealer was asked.

"Terrible," the old expert said.

"Are sales that bad?"

"Terrible."

"How long have they been terrible?" The veteran thought for a minute.

"Oh," he said. "About 51 years."

—*Robert M. Finlay*

Reformation

288   A young man told Dwight L. Moody, "I want to reform, but I don't know how to give up my undesirable friends." The evangelist answered, "That's easy. Just live a desirable life and your undesirable friends will give you up."

Restaurant

289   Man in a restaurant, looking at the menu: "Waiter, are any of these prices negotiable?"

—*Saturday Evening Post cartoon*

Retirement

290   Two weeks is about the ideal length of time to retire.

291   I had thought seriously of retirement at the age of 100, but I've upped it to 105.   —*Lowell Thomas*

292   Ain't no use in retiring, you just die faster.

—*George Miller*

Salaries

293 "What about comparative male/female pay scales,"
Mary Ayers, advertising executive, was asked. "If some
of the guys do the jobs that these girls are doing, they
can make the same money," she answered.

—*New Woman*

Sale

294 A man slightly under the influence of alcohol walked
into a bakery, ordered a chocolate cake, and then asked
for a knife and scraped off all the chocolate icing. Asked
the clerk, "Why didn't you buy a plain pound cake?"

The customer replied, "Because you have a special on
chocolate cakes. I always shop for the specials."

—*The Charlotte Weekly-East*

Salesman

295 The salesman who can think clearly, is imaginative, and
can act decisively hits the top.   —*George N. Kahn*

296 Someone I respect once pointed out to me: "The auto is
the device that enables salesmen to drive past three important prospects, to call on an insignificant client 30
miles away who could have been handled in a five-
minute phone call."   —*J. Porter Henry, Jr.*

297 A salesman who cannot close sales is not a salesman; he
is merely a conversationalist.   —*Charles B. Roth*

298 The buyer, being pressed by the salesman, said, "I'm
not going to buy today because the snowfall in New
Hampshire was too light last July."

The salesman quickly replied, "I thought I'd heard all
the objections ever stated but that's a new one on me.
What do you really mean?"

"I mean," the customer said, "if I'm not going to
buy, one excuse is as good as another."

—*Henri S. Laurent*

299 Frowning customer to salesman: "Yes, I admit you've
answered all my objections but one. I object to you."

300   It doesn't make any difference whether it's a man or woman doing the selling. A woman might get a second glance because of her sex, but it doesn't help in her sales. I have to work hard if I want to make some money.   *—Rose Heizman*

Second Career

301   People have more choices than they realize . . . You don't have to jump from one income to another in order to change your career. If you work eight hours a day at your present job and four hours at trying to build something else, that's building a future.
     —Isabelle K. Mewes

Self-confidence

302   Do not wish for self-confidence . . . get it from within . . . . Self-confidence comes to you every time you are knocked down and get up. A little boy was asked how he learned to skate. "Oh, by getting up every time I fell down," he replied.   *—Emerson*

Senior Citizen

303   Young man to his grandfather: "Grandfather, stop being such a gentleman!"
    Grandfather: "I *can't* stop. I've always been a gentleman."

304   As for Richard Rodgers' formula for keeping young, it is simply, "Work. Keep working. When you have something to do, it commands you."

Slavery

305   Below decks in a Roman galley . . . the slave-master addresses the slaves chained to their oars. "Slaves, the good news is that at the next port there will be food and grog for everyone. The bad news is that this afternoon the captain wants to go water skiing."   *—Newsweek*

Sleep

306   Don't sleep too much. If you sleep three hours less each night for a year, you will have an extra month and a half to succeed in.   *—Aristotle Onassis*

307   Pray that nobody finds a cure for insomnia. If science conquers that, there goes your last chance for a little privacy.   *—Changing Times*

Smoking

308   As a rule I have a lot of willpower. I gave up cigarettes with little effort. After six weeks locked in a closet, strapped to a chair listening to the recorded voice of Vincent Price saying over and over, "You do not want a cigarette," I quit cold turkey.   *—Ralph Reynolds*

Speech

309   President Woodrow Wilson was once asked how long he would prepare for a 10-minute talk. "Two weeks," he answered. "How long for an hour speech?" "One week," he said. "How long for a two-hour speech?" The president asserted, "I'm ready now."

310   A Washington newspaper reporter on the lecture circuit tells of this introduction, after a glowing biographical buildup, "And now, ladies and gentlemen, we'll hear the dope from Washington."

311   All men are sufficiently eloquent in that which they understand.   *—Socrates*

312   *(About Winston Churchill)*
He could carve a liquid waterfall of phrases out of desert rock.   *—Jim Bishop*

313   In handing the guest of honor a small package, the club president said, "The gift is small, so I'll have to make a big speech."   *—Cleo Lawrence*

314 I understand there are three kinds of speakers: name lecturers who get $1000 and up a lecture, speakers who are experts on a subject who earn $100 and up a speech, and the garden-variety talkers. Tonight I'm going to *talk* to you.

315 Discretion of speech is more than eloquence; and to speak agreeably to him with whom we deal is more than to speak in good words or in good order.   —*Bacon*

316 Basic rule for public speakers: Nice guys finish fast!

Sports

317 Sign on an ice-skating rink: "Have an ice time."

318 Coach to slow baseball runner: "You may march to a different drummer, but I want the beat speeded up."

319 *(After an unsuccessful baseball season)* "I'm going to write a book on my baseball career. It'll be 350 pages. All blank."   —*Joe Lis*

320 The only active sport which I follow is polo—and most of the work's done by the pony.   —*Prince Philip*

321 You call him a (football) passer? All he can pass is the buck.

322 Coach to crouched woman in tennis clothes, holding her racket in a press in playing position, ferocious expression: "Now, remember, Mrs. Townsend, what was the first thing we learned?"

323 A tennis player hit a ball off court and bent an antenna on a parked car. Contrite, the tennis player left a note offering to pay for the damage. The car owner phoned and said, "We're even-steven if you'll promise to use the money to take some tennis lessons."

324 Business is a combination of war and sport.
                                   —*Andre Maurois*

325 If all the year were playing holidays,
     To sport would be as tedious as to work.
                       —*Shakespeare, "King Henry IV"*

Success

326   When you see a man of the highest caliber, give thought to attaining his stature. When you see one who is not, go home and conduct a self-examination. —*Confucius*

327   Don't seek for haste, and don't concern yourself about small advantages. If you desire haste, you will not achieve success. If you have an eye to little advantages, the big things will not get done.   —*Confucius*

328   The great secret of success is to go through life as a man who never gets used up.   —*Albert Schweitzer*

329   The man who succeeds above his fellows is the one who early in life clearly discerns his object and toward that object habitually directs his powers.
                                            —*Edward G. Bulwer-Lytton*

330   A man must have a certain amount of intelligent ignorance to get anywhere.   —*Charles Kettering*

331   In success, ability is the punch, tact the deft foot-work.

332   *(Explaining how she became a bank vice-president)* Whatever I was asked to do, I did 10 times better than necessary.   —*Lynda Ferreri*

Surprise

333   I love surprises—as long as I'm ready for them.
                                            —*Beth S. Lenhart*

Switchboard

334   *(Woman at office switchboard)* This is Smith—grandmother's funeral, Keeler—strained ligament, Harrison—heavy cold, Gallagher—old war wound playing up, and Hayman—severe migraine . . . can I do anything for you?   —*Punch cartoon*

Tact

335   Tact: Tongue in check.   —*Arthur Glasow*

Teen-ager

336 A father saw his son slumped dejectedly in a living room chair on a Sunday, the picture of anguish and depression. He asked his wife, who was sitting nearby, "What calamity has struck our offspring?"

"He wants to go to the drugstore down at the corner," she said, "but the car won't start." —*Smiles*

337 My two teen-age daughters now negotiate with me. Every encounter is a negotiation. We negotiate all the time. I never knew there were so many negotiable items.
—*Mary Wells Lawrence*

Television

338 Most people thought television was impossible 30 years ago. Today a lot of people still do. —*Jobber Topics*

339 I hate television. I hate it as much as peanuts. But I can't stop eating peanuts. —*Orson Welles*

340 I'm waiting for the season's most realistic sit-com: Boy meets girl; boy loses girl; boy gets operation and *becomes* girl. —*S.F. Comedy Pool*

341 Television? It's my son's best friend.

342 I'll tell you how dull television is. Husbands have gone back to taking out the garbage.

Teeth

343 Adam and Eve had many advantages but the principal one was they escaped teething. —*Mark Twain*

Thanks

344 A really neglected form of compensation.
—*Robert Townsend*

Time

345 I erase as I go along. I look forward so much I have only an imperfect memory for the past. —*Thornton Wilder*

346   The past year couldn't have been all bad. First of all—it ended.

347   The past can teach you; the present can test you; the future can reward you.   *—Tarheel Wheels*

348   God makes people each in a special pattern. And in everyone He puts his own timetable.

349   Time should work for you, not you for time. It's the same as with money: you invest your time; you don't spend it.   *—Mark Silber*

Trouble

350   I have had a great many troubles in my life and most of them never happened.

Union

351   We've had the Ice Age, the Bronze Age and now the Union Age.

Universe

352   Our universe is such a perfect clock, I must get to know the watchmaker.   *—Voltaire*

Urban Sprawl

353   If you don't want to live in the city, pick a spot 10 miles beyond the outermost limits—and then go 50 miles further.   *—Frank Lloyd Wright*

Vacation

354   Of course you can enjoy a glorious vacation and stay within your budget. But not in the same summer.   *—Changing Times*

355   The one book that can tell you where to spend your vacation is your checkbook.   *—The Carolina Co-Operator*

Veterinarian

356 A veterinarian quit his practice and successfully ran for the legislature. One day in the middle of a heated debate, his opponent asked with a sneer: "Is it true that you're an animal doctor?"

"Indeed, it is," replied the veterinarian. "Are you ill?"

Volunteer

357 My basic philosophy, formed when I was in the army— "Never volunteer for anything."

358 "I'm volunteering so much now my husband reported me missing."   —*Erma Bombeck*

War

359 In its 200-year history, the United States has been to war nine times. This averages out to one every 22 years.   —*Jim Bishop*

360 Definition of the Bore War: The battle to rule the World of Explicit Sex.   —*Jo Foxworth*

Washington, DC

361 On an airline flight stopping at Washington, a stewardess asks if passengers will be going further or getting off at "Hot-Air Haven."
                              —*The Wall Street Journal*

362 This town is an island surrounded by a moat full of alligators.   —*David Brinkley*

Wedding

363 Father, watching his daughter select the most expensive wedding gown: "I don't mind giving you away, but must I gift-wrap you?"

Winning

364 I do not think winning is the most important thing. I think winning is the *only* thing.   —*Bill Veeck*

Wisdom

365 Wisdom is simply the scar tissue acquired from living.
                                                    —*Rolf Neill*

Wishes

366 It's not good for all your wishes to be fulfilled; through sickness you recognize the value of health; through evil, the value of good; through hunger, satisfaction; through exertion, the value of rest.   —*ACIPCO News*

Wit

367 Wit is the salt of the conversation not the food.
                                              —*William Hazlitt*

Women's Lib

368 The professions indeed supply the keystone to the arch of woman's liberty.   —*Julia Ward Howe*

369 ERA won't do anything for women. When you add it all up, it's a take-away of the rights women now have— the right of young women to avoid the draft, of women in the military to be free from combat, and of the wife to have the legal guarantee of support, provision of a home, and support for her minor children.
                                            —*Phyllis Schlafly*

370 Why don't we have more women in top positions? Because 20 years ago, we didn't put them into spots where they could start climbing the ladder.
                                                  —*Max Ulrich*

371 Clothes used to be number one in a woman's life, but now a woman prefers to be complimented on her accomplishments.   —*Marian Christy*

Work

372   When asked what gave him the most pleasure in life, Dr. Albert Schweitzer replied, "Whatever I am working at."

373   I don't like sitting on the patio as much as I did building the patio.   —*Miller Nichols*

374   Most of us find it difficult to get up in the morning—except on those days we don't have to.

—*Lane Olinghouse*

375   Some years ago, the head of a New York company put this message on the bulletin board: Some time between starting and quitting time, without infringing on lunch periods, coffee breaks, rest periods, story-telling, ticket-selling, holiday planning, and the rehashing of last night's TV programs, we ask that each employee try to find time for a work break. This may seem radical, but it might aid steady employment and assure regular paychecks.   —*Punch*

376   Office worker, holding phone, to colleague: "I eat an instant breakfast, come to work on rapid transit, and then spend the whole day on hold."   —*Mel Yalik*

377   During a recession a young man with a Ph.D. applied for a clerk's job at a real estate company. His interviewer was concerned that the Ph.D. might not be satisfied with such unchallenging work. "What would happen," he quizzed the candidate, "If your boss asked you to go get him a hamburger?"

The young man thought a minute and said, "I'd ask, 'Mustard and onion?' "

378   A statistician and his crew were adding up the final figures for a football game when a plane crashed into the stadium not far from where they were working. The statistician said, "Okay. Okay. Stare later. Right now we've got work to do."

379   Anyone can do any amount of work, provided it isn't the work he is supposed to be doing at that moment.

—*Robert Benchley*

380   If you're new and floundering around, at least learn to walk fast and carry lots of papers. This will make you look aggressive and industrious. It will also buy you some time, until you learn the ropes.   —*Andrea Farr*

381   Do a disagreeable job today instead of tomorrow. You will save 24 hours of dreading to do it while having 24 hours to savor the feeling that the job is behind you.

    —*Bob Talbert*

382   Had a chat with some young folks who are demanding meaningful employment, which turns out to be anything that brings happiness, fame, status and cash.

    —*Changing Times*

383   A boss and the personnel manager who hadn't had much luck in hiring someone for a low-paying receptionist's job were discussing what they wanted in a candidate.

"Which would you like best," said the personnel manager, "Brains, experience, or appearance?"

"Appearance," said the boss, "And the sooner the better!"

Working Mother

384   Returning to work, a mother was asked in a job interview about who would care for her five children. She said she had live-in help but neglected to say she was the live-in help.

385   Did you ever know a mother who didn't work?

Youth

386   Now they're making TVs small enough to fit into a hand. Great. Next time your kid holds his hand out, just put a TV in it.

387   The young are so busy teaching us they have no time to learn from us.

    —*Edmond G. Addeo and Robert E. Burger*

Acknowledgments

I wish to thank all whose remarks are quoted in
this book. Specifically I thank the following:

Advertising Age, panel discussion, May 10, 1976, quote by Ira C.
Herbert. *Agency Sales,* January 1976, quote by Frank Butrick. *American
Dry Cleaner,* January 1974, quote by columnist Marcia Miller. *American
Glass Review,* Clifton, N.J. March 1974, quote by George N. Kahn.
American Management Association, Inc., *The Management Evolution* by
Lawrence A. Appley, passage on p. 7 of foreword (by Clarence Francis), ©
1956 by American Management Association, Inc. *American Painting
Contractor,* excerpt from article.

Bicycle Journal, May 1976, quote by publisher Bill Quinn. *The Char-
lotte Observer,* September 26, 1976, quote by Charles Lloyd in column by
Dannye Romine, book editor. *The Chicago Tribune,* quote by Mary Wells
Lawrence in a feature story by Carol Kleinman. *The Chicago Tribune
Magazine,* October 10, 1976, quote by Herb. Daniels. *The Christian
Science Monitor,* May 24, 1976, quote by Lucia Mouat; October 26, 1976,
poem by Paul Armstrong; October 27, 1976, excerpt from "Why NYU Got
Out of Noodles," by Ron Scherer; reprinted by permission from *The Chris-
tian Science Monitor,* © 1976, The Christian Science Publishing Society. All
rights reserved. *Egospeak* by Edmond G. Addeo and Robert E. Burger, ©
by the authors. Excerpt reprinted with the permission of the publisher,
Chilton Book Company, Radnor, PA.

The Dial Press, quote from *The Overachievers* by Peter H. Engel, © by
author.

Marc Engeler, quote from an address to Daycroft. The Honorable Sam
J. Ervin, Jr., two quotes.

Field Newspaper Syndicate, © two quotes by Sydney J. Harris. *Fortune
Magazine,* May 1976, quote by Arthur M. Louis.

Harper & Row, *Inside Africa* by John Gunther, one quote; *How to Develop Your Executive Ability,* by Daniel Starch, quote: Hawthorn Books, Inc., *A Treasury of Success Unlimited.* Og Mandino, quote. Dr. Robert L. Heilbroner, quote. *Home Life,* November 1975, © 1975, The Sunday School Board of the Southern Baptist Convention, quote by Oren Arnold. All rights reserved. Used by permission. Houghton Mifflin Company, *Ambassador's Journal,* John Kenneth Galbraith, quote.

Lee A. Iacocca, excerpt from speech before the *Sales Executives Club of New York,* September 10, 1971.

Jeno's Credos, Jeno F. Paulucci, quote.

Alfred A. Knopf, Inc., *Up the Organization,* © Robert Townsend, two quotes.

Isabelle K. Mewes, quote. Modern Maturity, October-November 1974, quote by Martha Graham.

The National Enquirer, quote. *Nation's Business,* 1975, quote from article by Stuart Atkins and Allan Katcher. *New Woman,* quote by Mary Ayres from article by Robert S. Berman, September-October 1973; quote by Jeffrey Feinman, May-June 1976. *North Carolina Magazine,* August 1976, quote by Charles E. Hayworth.

Parade Magazine, May 25, 1975, quote by Phyllis Schlafly. *Parents' Magazine,* October 1976, James Farmer, quote. Prentice-Hall Inc., *Secrets of Closing Sales,* by Charles B. Roth, © 1970, quote; *How to Cash In on Your Abilities,* by Dora Albert, © 1961, quote; How I Raised Myself from Failure to Success in Selling, by Frank Bettger, © 1949, two quotes; *The Twelve Hats of a Company President,* by Willard F. Rockwell, Jr., © 1971. *Public Relations News,* quote by editor Denny Griswold. *Publication International Ltd. New Job Opportunities for Women,* by Muriel Lederer and the editors of Consumer Guide (R), © 1975, quote.

Dr. Jung Bay Ra, quote from article in *Journal of Social Psychology,* June 1977.

Simon & Schuster, *Management Through People, by Dale Carnegie & Associates, quote.*

The Southern Pines Pilot, essay by Kathy Power, quoted in column by Sam Ragan.

Time, © Time Inc., June 12, 1972, quote by Charles Kemmans Wilson.

U.S. Tobacco Journal, June 5, 1975, quote by Rose Heizman.

Ward's Auto World, March 1976, quote.